HOW TO WRITE
ATTENTION-GRABBING
QUERY &
COVER
LETTERS

JOHN WOOD

WRITER'S DIGEST BOOKS
Cincinnati, Ohio

How to Write Attention-Grabbing Query & Cover Letters. Copyright © 1996 by John Wood. Printed and bound in the United States of America. All rights reserved. No part of this book may be reproduced in any form or by any electronic or mechanical means including information storage and retrieval systems without permission in writing from the publisher, except by a reviewer, who may quote brief passages in a review. Published by Writer's Digest Books, an imprint of F&W Publications, Inc., 1507 Dana Avenue, Cincinnati, Ohio 45207. (800) 289-0963. First edition.

This hardcover edition of *How to Write Attention-Grabbing Query & Cover Letters* features a "self-jacket" that eliminates the need for a separate dust jacket. It provides sturdy protection for your book while it saves paper, trees and energy.

Other fine Writer's Digest Books are available from your local bookstore or direct from the publisher.

00 99 98 97 96   5 4 3 2 1

Library of Congress Cataloging-in-Publication Data

Wood, John
     How to write attention-grabbing query & cover letters / John Wood.
          p.   cm.
     Includes bibliographical references (p.) and index.
     ISBN 0-89879-704-7 (alk. paper)
     1. Letter writing. 2. English language—Rhetoric. I. Title.
PE1483.W58   1996
808.6′0248—dc20   95-52870
                                                                CIP

Edited by Jack Heffron and Roseann Biederman
Cover design by Brian Roeth

To Mr. Taubman, who first saw my talent and let me run with it.
And to Lucy and Alex, who understood what I wanted to do.

About the Author

John Wood has been a senior editor at *Modern Maturity* since 1983 where he has read, in his estimation, more than 25,000 query letters. From 1989 to 1991, he also served as an editorial consultant for Newcastle Publishing Company, where he helped conceive and edit the "Looking Forward Collection," a new line of books geared to people over fifty.

He has lectured to writer's organizations, has been a judge for various writer's contests and has served as a consultant to the Writer's Digest School. His articles have appeared in *Basketball Digest*, *Newsday*, the *Miami Herald*, *Writer's Digest* and *Writer's Market*. He lives in Los Angeles.

Acknowledgments

I want to thank a number of people who were instrumental in helping to conceive and complete this project. First of all, I want to thank my former editor and current publisher, Bill Brohaugh, whose faith and support of my work has never wavered. Next come my editorial colleagues at *Modern Maturity*, whose help with and approval and encouragement of my work was of immense comfort and reassurance. Special thanks also go to Roseann Biederman, Jack Heffron, Susan Goodman, Russell Galen, David Hale Smith and each of the writers who let me showcase their queries in my book. And, of course, I can't forget the many, many editors over the years whose offhand "not bad" or "try me again" scribbled on a reject letter kept me writing and dreaming. As you inspired me to continue, I now hope to inspire others.

But most of all, I wish to thank *you*, the writer. It is, after all, your words and ideas and zest for this wonderful profession that enable me to keep doing what I love to do. To all of your who have inspired, excited or astonished me by your queries (or will in the future), I have only one thing to say: "Keep your ideas coming—as long as they're accompanied by an SASE!"

TABLE OF CONTENTS

Introduction

In early 1984, sometime during my first week on the job as the newly
hired senior editor of *Dynamic Years* (the former sister magazine of *Modern Maturity*, where I now reside), I was given a manila folder so thick that
only a gigantic rubber band could keep its contents from spilling across my
desk. "Great!" I said eagerly, not knowing what the file contained but eager
to tackle it nevertheless. I didn't care. I was a bona fide editor; I was working
at a real magazine; I was working with writers and publishers and agents.
Nothing they could put in front of me could possibly dampen my enthusiasm.

The person who'd given me the folder just looked at me as if to say,
"You poor, pitiful wretch—how naive can you be?"

I opened the folder and out fell a loose stack of letters and manuscripts
and photographs and envelopes and stamps and . . . and then it hit me. This
was the dreaded "slush-pile" I'd read so much about when I used to freelance. This was my first batch of query letters. These letters used to be mine.
These were writers whose hopes and dreams were now in my hands. And I
had the key—I could buy any one of them, or all of them.

And then I read the first one.

I don't remember what it was about, but I do remember it wasn't bad,
which surprised me. I'd expected it to be awful—scribbled on a grocery sack
with a crayon or something—because of what I'd heard from other editors.
I read another one. And another. When I finished the pile, I was both relieved and disappointed. Relieved because the chore had not been sheer
drudgery; most of the letters were similar in quality: they were all pretty
much in the ballpark. In fact, I found the experience invigorating. I had faith
that each submission might turn up the next unheralded writer, the next
great idea, the next National Magazine Award. Being a writer myself, I
rooted silently for each letter to be a saleable one. Although my expectations
today are considerably lower as a result of wading through the slush-pile for
so long, I still tacitly urge on every query letter put before me.

What disappointed me on that first day, however, was that so many of
the letters were fool's gold; they were so *close* to being the real thing. Remarkably, that situation still holds true today. The vast majority of the twenty-
five thousand query letters I've read to date have been rejected, mostly be-

cause their authors made the same simple mistakes I found in that initial batch tossed onto my desk more than twelve years ago.

Imagine you, like me, are reading such a stack of query letters. From writers very similar to you—homemakers, salespersons, students, waiters, truckers, secretaries, ad execs, retirees—real people living in (I'm leafing through an actual pile now) Vineyard Haven, MA; Albuquerque, NM; Jonesboro, GA; Monroe, CT; Cold Spring Harbor, NY; West Hills, CA. All of their hopes riding on their letter—addressed to you.

And they blow it.

What really riles you, though, is you can see at a glance *why* they blew it. So why don't *they* see it?

That's why I wrote this book. To serve as the ultimate user's manual for freelance writers—the guide I never had when I was starting out. A checklist of what to do—and what not to do—when composing practically any kind of writing-related correspondence. In short, a primer on how to become a professional. I know how hard it is to write letters, how passionate about an idea someone can get, and how much it means for a beginning writer to see his or her byline in print. I've been there. It means everything.

As a writer, I labored for years sending queries to magazines, cocksure that my ideas would captivate every editor I sent them to. When most of them came back with little more than a "Thank you," I was more perplexed than hurt. How can this be? What am I doing wrong? (Everything, it turned out, but I didn't know that—writers never get any feedback.) So, like most freelancers, I kept making the same mistakes over and over again—and kept getting rejected over and over again.

Well, no more. By the time you finish this book, I guarantee that your writing sales will improve. And I don't mean a little—I mean *a lot*. As I mentioned previously, most query letters aren't that far off the mark; a few minor adjustments are usually all that's needed to fine-tune your technique—and start earning money. Consider this book your toolbox and owner's manual; all you have to do is make the calibrations.

What's in This Book

Other books have been written on how to write query letters, but this one delves deeper. Rather than paint the topic with a broad brush (how to research and generate article and book ideas, how to find markets, how to sell and slant your work), this book assumes you already know how and what to write. Instead, it's much more focused, concentrating on the details and mechanics of letter-writing itself. It shows you how to put your concept on paper in a way that will hit every magazine or book editor's hot button—and avoid every one of their kill buttons.

It explains, for example the ten positive things editors look for in query letters (the Ten Query Commandments) and the ten negative things editors hate to find (the Ten Query Sins). What goes through a writer's mind when he writes a query? What goes through an editor's mind when she reads one? What gratifies a book editor when he goes over a book proposal? What upsets an agent when she scrutinizes a cover letter? Each of these issues are analyzed in detail on the following pages.

The book begins with a look back at the lost art of correspondence, at a time when penning one's hopes and thoughts and ventures—one's life—on paper to a friend or loved one was the highlight of the day, week or month. An era when the joy of writing was so innate that it caused Francis Quarles to jot down in one of his missives, "I wish thee as much pleasure in the reading as I had in the writing."

Not so today. Just finding the time to write a thank-you note, let alone a two-page letter, seems impossible, and the actual composing—sheer agony! What's happened to this once-cherished activity? Actually, not a whole lot, as it turns out. Pens, ink and paper still abound, as do friends, relatives and lovers. The problem is, we have more convenient and compelling alternatives to letters these days. As a result, letter-writing has gone out of style—and we've lost the knack.

For writers, this is good news and bad news. The bad news is, your success hinges on letter-writing know-how, so if you've fallen out of favor with it, you're dead. The good news is, the fact that you're a writer makes it unlikely you've slipped very far. As a writer, you know, for instance, that not all writing is pleasurable, but once you get into it—once you're "in the zone," to use a pro athlete's expression—even the most tedious writing project can suddenly turn galvanizing and before you know it, your words are flying off the page. In the first chapter I show how to recapture the thrill you get from reading and writing a great letter—and how to transfer that electricity into your day-to-day query-writing regimen.

We next move on to the heart of the book—the chapters on article queries, nonfiction book queries and novel queries—even advice and information on how to prepare what some writers deem the most trying tests of all: nonfiction book proposals and novel synopses.

But writers don't live off queries alone, as you know. You're required to send out many different types of letters—before, during and after your assignments. These specialized letters can be just as crucial to the success of your projects as the original queries themselves. One chapter, for example, is devoted to writing cover letters (short, introductory notes accompanying manuscripts that don't require query letters, e.g., short stories, humor and essays). Another chapter explains how to master all the other miscellaneous letters that writers are commonly called upon to crank out (follow-up letters, assignment-acceptance letters, negotiation letters, update letters, rewrite letters—plus letters to agents, publishers, publicists, PR agencies, etc.).

At the end of each chapter, a lively Q & A section tackles issues related to that particular form of letter.

A unique angle of this book, in addition to demonstrating letter-writing fundamentals, is its tone. Each step throughout this guide, you are given counsel and tips from two perspectives (twin muses, if you will). One voice is from the writer's point of view: What are your priorities and expectations regarding writing and selling, and what are your needs, concerns and misconceptions regarding editors? The other voice is from the editor's point of view: What are our priorities and expectations regarding reading and buying, and what are our needs, concerns and misconceptions regarding you?

Both voices help illustrate why writers and editors often have misconceptions about the other, show that they often have similar passions, worries and conflicts, and explain that if the writer wants to succeed he must try to get inside the mind-set of an editor. And that if the editor wants to succeed she must show compassion for writers by getting inside *their* heads, too. Since I've been both a magazine writer/editor and book writer/editor, I know intimately what each is going through during the crucial and fragile query-writing stage of the writer/editor relationship.

How important is knowing what the "other side" thinks? I can't tell you how many times during my early freelancing days I wanted to just chuck it all (my writing, not my life). Then I'd see a note scribbled on the bottom of a reject letter that said: "Can't use it—all stocked up—but your tale of the One Chicken Inn on Moorea sure brought back memories." I mean, it meant the world. That lone editor sitting in that faraway office may not have known it (or maybe he did; and if so, I'm eternally grateful) but he kept me going for another year, minimum.

More important, *he did not have to do that*. Being an editor now, I know how much trouble such a gesture takes sometimes. Jotting down an encouraging note to a beginning writer isn't as easy as it looks. You are dealing with an extremely fragile ego whose confidence (like mine years ago) may be near the breaking point. Every word must be chosen with care. You can say the wrong thing; you can say too much and unleash a furious rebuttal, which was not your intention; or you can open up a Pandora's box and end up on this guy's mailing list for life. All have happened to me. I, therefore, labor over these comments long and hard. Needless to say, the editor/writer relationship is a unique one that not much has been written about . . . until now.

Which leads me to mention the chapter ("The Writer and the Editor") devoted exclusively to this relationship. The first part is written "From the Writer's Desk," the second part "From the Editor's Desk." The former describes what a typical writer goes through as he composes a query, showing how he thinks the editor will react upon receiving his letter (and how she really does). The latter describes what a typical editor goes through as she reads a query, showing what the editor expects the writer to write (and what she really gets). If you've always wondered what editors do and how they think, don't miss this section. Conversely, if you've always wanted to know what editors *really* think of you, check it out.

But perhaps the most interesting and helpful aspect of this book are the letters themselves—nearly fifty sample letters are interspersed throughout the text. Some are mock queries designed to illustrate ideal and mistake-prone versions that I've laid out so you can refer to them again and again like a checklist. They are dissected paragraph by paragraph, with margin notes explaining their particular strengths and weaknesses. The bulk of the letters, however, are bunched near the end of most chapters. These are actual letters from freelance writers that resulted in either sales or near-sales, or I've cited them because of the exemplary nature of what they set out to accomplish.

This Is Your Book

Finally, I wrote this book (the book I wish I'd had when I was a beginning writer twenty years ago) for you. I want you to succeed, to do what you were destined to do. I want you to know what you're doing right and wrong with your queries so you can improve your techniques and break down the barriers that this crazy publishing industry has built up to separate the wheat from the chaff.

The writing profession is a cruel and unfair catch-22 situation. You can't prove to us editors your ideas are ideal for us and you're the perfect person to do them unless you actually write the pieces. But we won't let you write them (won't even read them in most cases) unless you query us first. Teeth-gnashing aside, those are the rules, so your only recourse is to ensure that your query letters are better prepared, targeted and written than those of your competitors.

The good news is: Most of your competitors' query letters aren't very good. You, on the other hand, are reading this book.

So, this is my pledge: If you're serious about being a professional writer (e.g., writing to sell as opposed to writing for fun) and if you heed the guidelines outlined on the following pages, I can assure you that you will avoid all magazine, publisher and agent slush-piles from this day forward. Not only that, but your submissions will wind up in the in-basket of the most appropriate individual at every institution you send them to.

How important are these two accomplishments? Immeasurably so—fewer than ten percent of all freelancers, in my estimation, can do it. Once the secrets outlined in this guidebook become second nature to you, don't be surprised if your future letters start producing some of your best writing—not to mention bylines and checks.

Good luck. Let me know when that happens.

CHAPTER ONE

The Art of Correspondence

"An odd thought strikes me: We shall receive no letters in the grave."
Dorothy Osborne

When was the last time you sat down and wrote a long, leisurely hand-written missive to a friend, relative or loved one—or received one? (And no, I'm not talking about that form letter the Fergusons send to everybody at Christmas.) Why is that Chinese-lacquered fountain pen ol' Grand-dad gave you gathering dust in the rosewood box of mementos you keep in the hall closet? How come the only time we use pen and ink anymore is to sign (oh, excuse me, that's asking too much—to *initial*) a memo to the boss? And has anyone noticed that practically our only remaining methods of communication among the species—the embodiment of twentieth-century interaction—are phone, voice mail, E-mail, junk mail, form letter, postcard, Post-it, pager, fax, modem or Internet?

The honorable art of letter writing is dead. It has fallen out of favor. We've lost the hang of it. What killed such a pleasant diversion? I suspect it's that we have easier, faster ways of communicating today than we used to. Writing letters, once one of our more popular leisure pursuits and an integral part of our lives, plummeted seemingly overnight to the bottom of our activity list. It's no longer a pleasure but an intrusion.

Today we're making quota if we squeeze out an occasional postcard to a long-distance relative or a friend once a month, and then only if we "have time." And if we're freelance writers? Hah, forget it—we'll call you, we'll do lunch, we'll drive cross-country to say "Hi" before *we* drop anything in the mail. Writing letters is what we do twelve hours a day. And judging by the number of ones we get rejected, about eleven hours and fifty-nine minutes of our time amounts to zip.

It never used to be that way. Writer Vivian Gornick, in a 1994 essay in the *New York Times Book Review*, recalls an earlier era when the whole world seemed to be writing letters: "It was the accustomed way of ordinarily educated people to occupy the world beyond their own small and immediate lives. . . . At home the phone rang only rarely and the television set was hardly ever on. The apartment was richly quiet. If you had a taste for your own thoughts it wasn't difficult to pursue them, and if you wanted to connect over them—talk, reflect, enlarge upon with a sympathetic or kindred spirit—you sat down and wrote a letter.

"I loved ordering my thoughts, savoring the agenda. What did I want to say, and in what order would I say it? How would I arrange fact and impression . . . : describe a mood, pass on information, . . . build an atmosphere on the page larger than the facts? Writing a letter was a greater pleasure than receiving one."

When I was in the army in the late 1960s I was stationed in Vietnam. Partly because fax machines and on-line services were nonexistent and phoning home was out of the question, and partly because I loved to write and was dying to tell everybody what was happening there, I dashed off boxes and boxes of letters. Ten- and twenty-page letters, the kind mothers love. The last time I looked, my folks still had them, too, packed away in one dusty corner of the garage. Ah, the good old days.

I'm ashamed to admit it, but I rarely write personal letters anymore. I could say that's because my adventures are less exotic these days and I have nowhere near the free time I had then. But in fact, I loathe the time, effort and obligation the exercise demands—and the guilt that builds up from this abnormal aversion. Naturally, a reluctance to write personal letters can cause serious problems for people who have to write query letters to make a living.

When I started freelance writing many years ago, I was advised by several writers and editors to "Get a nighttime job that offers plenty of quiet time to write, or an easy day job so you won't be too exhausted to write when you get home." Then they added, "And don't take any job that involves writing. If you do, the last thing you'll want to do when you get home is grind out a 5,000-word article on tomato farming or, heaven forbid, a novel."

What they forgot to mention was that in order to *publish* what I wrote, I would first have to send out letters—lots of them, which could amount to nearly as much writing as a full-time writing job would. If I spent most of my time crafting letters, I could burn myself out. If I spent little time letter-writing, I'd sell zilch. Result: Partly because I had gotten out of the habit of writing letters, partly because I was suddenly forced to write so many of them, and partly because queries are so bloody difficult, my flair for correspondence diminished, shall we say, considerably.

Writing to thank Aunt Zelda for your Christmas sweater is hard enough if you've lost the ardor, but having to pitch an editor when you're in a letter-writing funk has to be the unholiest of pursuits. You're being judged by a peer, not an intimate; your words are being critiqued, not cherished; your thought isn't what counts, only your information. No wonder so many writers despair at writing query letters—and why so many editors dread reading them.

The Secret to Writing Great Letters

The essence of all great letters—all great writing—is the same: Energy, information, informality and surprise. A personal letter with each of these will be memorable. *And so will a query.* If you want your queries to be special, therefore, instill them with the same "oomph" that you put into your letters to mom or your old dorm roommate.

I'm not talking about a major difference in the way you write. The words and phrasing in good query letters aren't that much different from those in mediocre ones. What sets the better ones apart are subtle distinctions in tone: They're a tad more spirited, more earnest, more compelling—without being gushy or gaga. The best letters are written by those who seem to get a rush out of doing what their unsuccessful peers clearly dread. They don't treat the task as a tedious chore; they relish it as an opportunity to strut their stuff. Their attitude is: "Oh boy, another chance to jaw about one of the greatest ideas I've come up with—to someone who's dying to hear it."

What happened the last time you saw a great movie or read a fabulous book? I'll tell you what happened: You couldn't wait to tell someone about it. I don't have to tell *you* the joy you get in that telling (if you don't enjoy it, you're in the wrong business). Well, that's all a query is. Good queries, like good storytellers, grab your attention and hold it; poor ones just make you shrug, "So what?" Unfortunately, too many writers drain much of the enthusiasm from their queries, believing that the more dry and formal their pages look, the more professional they will appear. Instead, it just makes them look like dull professionals. Don't blot the vitality from your queries; soak 'em in the sweat and blood of your convictions. Choose delight over despair and let your muse prevail. As Robert Frost wrote, "No tears in the writer, no tears in the reader."

Do you remember the most memorable personal letter you ever received? What made it so extraordinary? I'll bet, first of all, it started out with a bang:

"You'll never guess who just got married!"

That's because nobody wants to wade through polite preliminaries (yawn) at the beginning of a letter. Readers want to get to the goods. That's true of both Aunt Ethel and Editor Susan—with one important exception. Although both recipients are just as eager to learn what's on your mind, only Aunt Ethel will tolerate a long-winded intro (and I'm cutting Ethel a lot of slack here).

Second, each paragraph was most likely short and contained a brand-new tidbit:

"The high-school reunion was a hoot. . . ."

"Pooch chased that damn yellow Buick again and is back at the vet's. . . ."

"How 'bout them 49ers, eh? . . ."

You may know more about what you're writing than anyone else, but nobody will care if you take forever to say it, don't say it clearly, or don't present it persuasively. Good queries aren't dissertations, they're short, punchy telegrams of astonishment.

And third, it undoubtedly read like the person was talking to you in person. That means it did not start off with: "As per your request dated 4/21/96. . . . " or "Pursuant to your previous letter. . . ." Chances are it began with:

"I'm sorry."

Or: *"Yo, weasel-butt, remember me?—Spooner, from 4th Battalion!"*

Or: *"I hope you don't mind but I live in the same building and notice that each day when you pass by my window on the way to the mailbox, my day brightens considerably—and I was wondering if we could meet so I could confirm if it's you . . . or just the time of day that's doing it.*

Thank you,

Woman in Apt. 3b."

In other words, the more any letter sounds like you're talking to the reader—the more it sounds like *you*—the more effective it'll be. *So will a query.* A query is the only way the editor can size up who you are and how your mind works. Editors are human, too. They like to feel they're dealing with a real person—not a form letter—someone who sees them as a real person, too.

That said, from this day forward you will have no excuse for ever starting a query this way again: "Enclosed please find a query on Chicago that I believe would be of particular interest to your readers for the following reasons. . . ."

Instead, it should go out this way:

"Think you know Chicago? I bet you don't. In fact, I'll prove it. What's the first thing that comes to mind when you think of Chicago? Stop. *You're humming* My Kind of Town, *aren't you? Well, this bulletin's just in: You—and the Chairman of the Board—are outa touch, pal. Read on, and I'll tell you what Chicago really is and why your readers ought to know about it. This is Chicago.* Today's *Chicago.* Now *Chicago. And it's like nothin' you—or Ol' Blue Eyes—ever saw before. . . ."*

If you think this kind of approach seems too risky to send to an unknown editor, you are being too squeamish in your query letters. Believe me, safe, formal, unadventurous letters will go nowhere—except right back to you. The last thing you want to mull over is, "Hmm, is this too dicey to send out?" If you're the skittish type, I refer you to what Paul Newman said to Robert Redford in *Butch Cassidy and the Sundance Kid* after Redford, as Cassidy, balked at jumping off a cliff into a river to escape the posse because he couldn't swim: "Hell, the fall *alone'll* kill ya."

I have news for you: *Every* query letter is chancy, whether it's from a raw beginner or a seasoned pro. Even if you do everything right—according to this book's recommendations, someone else's or your own—your odds of getting an assignment to a major newsstand magazine are still paltry when you consider all the obstacles and factors that are out of your and even top professionals' control (such as an editor's personal likes and dislikes, indecision, whimsy, cluelessness, slothfulness, idiocy, or not-really-giving-a-hootness). So, given those odds, what have you got to lose? Go for it. Take some chances.

Athletes and teams who aren't expected to win often perform better than they ever have, and sometimes produce stunning upsets, simply because the pressure's off. That same principle can work for you, too. In the writing profession, freelance writers certainly have to be considered the underdog. But that doesn't stop a few odd rookies now and then from stepping up to the plate with their cap askew, their eyes queer, their stance crooked and their disposition jiggly. Instead of safely bunting to move the man over, they ignore the odds, disdain the coach's signs, and swing with abandon. Occasionally, one of them will get all the wood on the ball—and from that moment, his rookie days are over.

The Write Stuff

In *The Right Stuff*, Tom Wolfe chronicles America's space program and its first astronauts. The underlying theme of the American Book Award winner was how extraordinary were those first men selected for the inaugural Mercury missions. They were the best of the best in every category—fitness, intelligence, nerves, zeal. They prided themselves on "pushing the envelope," as they called it, farther than anyone else. A test pilot's job was to see how far he could push the most dangerous jet prototypes in existence—before the aircraft's aerodynamic envelopes literally burst. Many, many pilots died. The scientists, the military and the government, however, needed desperately to know how much these thousand-ton metal missiles could take under the most severe conditions. The findings, they prayed, would one day lead man to the moon, reap a scientific breakthrough, help turn the tide in battle, or maybe even prevent a war. The bolder the pilots got, the higher up the ladder they climbed.

Do you see where I'm going with this? In a way, you're pushing the envelope, too—your SASE—every time you send out a query. Only a small percentage of freelance-writer test pilots ever succeed. What are they doing at the wheel that you're not? If you're still stuck at ground level in your writing career, take a hard look under the engine—at the correspondence you're sending out. Most likely, that's where the smoke's coming from.

Are your submission takeoffs timid, or are they daring? Do you send them off gliding on auto-pilot, or do you steer each one solo? Is your handling safe and steady, or does it allow for a barrel-roll or 360 now and then? And finally, are you flying, not because you particularly enjoy it, but because it's the quickest way to get from point A to point B—or are you up there because it sets you free, because you're on you're own, and because you can do and go whatever and wherever the hell you want to?

My point is, if you want your sales to soar, your queries had better have the write stuff. And the only way I know to accomplish that is by rediscovering the pleasure of letter-writing. Take more chances, express more feelings, evoke more emotions, draw more gasps. Vow to never send out another query again—from this day forward your letters to editors will be *personal*. You should write them in such a way that the fortunate recipients recognize, from the opening line, that you're on to something startling and that you're not the typical hack.

Once you've rejuvenated the humdrum query process, stand back and watch what happens. You'll start knocking out queries the way you were born to write, the way you want to write, the way you naturally write—not the way you think you're expected to write—and, what's more, you'll start to like it! Then you'll be on course to earning your wings and landing those all-important assignments.

It doesn't take much to master the art of query writing. You just have to enjoy life and yourself—and have an insatiable desire to tell the world about the former via the latter. Everything else flows from that. As Oliver Wendell Holmes, Jr., once said, "The best test of truth is the power of the thought to get itself accepted in the competition of the market." As long as each letter you send is sealed with passion and professionalism, you will never have to worry about the competition.

CHAPTER TWO

The Writer and the Editor

"We have a failure to communicate."
from *Cool Hand Luke*

Making cold calls to strangers by mail (which freelancers have to do) and replying to cold calls from strangers by form letters (which editors have to do) will never make it as exhibits in the Great Communication Hall of Fame, if one is ever constructed. Yet this is how writers and editors do business with each other. No wonder it's so hard to sell your writing.

There's got to be a better way.

There is. It's called empathy. It's called understanding. If more editors sympathized with what writers go through, they would respect—not reject—query letters for what they are. And if more writers empathized with what editors go through, the general quality of query letters would improve—which in turn would lessen the chances of rejection.

Am I dreaming? Well, let's find out. I'm dividing this chapter into two sections: "From the writer's desk" and "From the editor's desk." The former will describe what a typical writer goes through as he creates, researches and composes a query. The latter will describe what a typical editor goes through as she reads, analyzes, and decides whether to pursue or reject a query.

Both sections will discuss why writers and editors often have misconceptions about the other; show that they often have similar passions, stresses, worries, and conflicts; and explain that if the writer wants to succeed he must operate like a professional and try to get inside the mind-set of an editor—and that if the editor wants to succeed she must have compassion for writers and try to see where *they're* coming from, too.

Since all queries begin with you, the writer, let's go to your desk first.

Although this section deals mainly with what you do and may, on the surface, appear superfluous, I advise you to read it anyway—and read it closely—because it contains special insights into your work life and thought processes that may benefit—and surprise—many of you, especially those just starting out.

From the Writer's Desk

It's been a busy and weary—and typical—day for freelance writer Bob, who works nine-to-five at a public-relations firm spinning out press releases. He rose at 5:00 A.M. to give him time, before going to work, to put the finishing touches on the third rewrite of his article on scuba diving in Cancun that a cruise-magazine editor wants redone by the end of the week—even though the editor still doesn't know exactly what's wrong with it (all she could muster was: "It needs a little more punch in the middle and a couple of graphs somewhere to enhance the overall mood").

At lunchtime Bob again puts on his freelance writer's hat and, while wolfing down a tuna sandwich at his desk, spends the next forty-five minutes sweating blood composing two letters—one a cover letter to accompany a poignant Christmas memory of his father that he wants to submit to *Reader's Digest*, and one a query on how to scalp a ticket scalper that he must customize for six different sports publications. Then he makes copies, attaches an SASE to each, and sends them all to the post office. At 5:00 P.M. he leaves the office and rushes to the local library, where he spends a couple of hours researching a potential future article on the five most common sleep disorders among women that he hopes will pique the interest of one of the top women's magazines. At 7:15, exhausted and hungry, Bob finally heads home, nukes a TV dinner in the microwave, and works for another hour-and-a-half on his Great American Novel. Remembering that he forgot to check the mail, he sleepwalks to the mailbox and surveys the damage: seven SASEs returned (all rejects), his Howard Stern parody to *Playboy* is back already (hadn't he mailed it just last week?), two postcards from Hollywood agents saying "Thanks, but no thanks" to his TV script, and a note scribbled from an editor saying his Machu Picchu query "sounds intriguing"—but could she see it on spec?

It's days like this when many writers wonder whatever possessed them to launch a writing career in the first place or what made them ever think they had even the remotest bit of talent to become a successful writer. Bob is not one of these writers. He's wondering about something else. He's trying to imagine what sad state of affairs could possibly have allowed so many incompetents to rise to such lofty editing positions.

Why can't editors recognize true talent? Why can't editors see what's best for their own magazine? Why can't editors make up their bloody minds? Bob loves being a writer and loves the stimulation and challenge it brings, and can't wait to celebrate when he finally sells his first piece. But until he finds an editor who knows what he or she wants—and can explain it clearly and concisely—that vintage bottle of port he's been waiting to pop will have to keep.

But not for long. The absolute certainty of that in Bob's mind is what keeps him writing every single day, without exception, no matter how many rejections his words produce. He keeps reminding himself that he is simply in a state of "freelancer's purgatory," a normal but temporary learning and growing phase—OK, a rut—that every beginning writer goes through. He also knows, from reading about writing and talking to many writers and editors, that successful writers didn't become successful because they were necessarily better writers than anyone else; they got where they were because they didn't quit during this most trying ordeal. So Bob keeps his head up, his pen scribbling, and his dream of sales and success alive.

Soon, he knows, he will hit it big. He will sell The Article. He will break out of Freelance Novel, Tennessee. And until he does, he's doing what he can't help but do—write. Bob isn't any different from anyone else. He knows he's better than most editors give him credit for. He doesn't belong in *Lawn & Landscape* or *The Journal of Meteorology and Science* or the *Boise Gazette and Star News* any more than John Grisham does (actually, John Grisham does belong there, but that's a whole other issue). Bob knows in his gut he's *this* far from being in *Esquire*, in *Redbook*, in *Rolling Stone*. He's seen his byline and author's photo there, he's read his article there, he's by God already critiqued his layout there. The only thing keeping him from actually *being* there is for one editor to say "Yes" instead of "No." That's all.

Then Bob will be *one of them*. A plain notecard will arrive shortly afterward in the mail, unsigned, no return address. A meeting place and time will be embossed on the card in bold Times Roman script. He will arrive appropriately late. There, in hushed darkness, along with numerous other freelancers who've been anointed The Gift, he'll be initiated. Probably in the bowels of some hallowed institution like the Condé Nast building, presided over by the likes of Brendan Gill or, if she feels like getting out, Joyce Carol Oates. I don't think there's any point bringing up Robert James Waller here.

He'll be given the secret handshake that, according to his instructions, only real writers are to slip each other when mingling at Tina Brown cocktail parties. Within days, editors will begin calling him. "How did you get my number?" Bob will ask naively. There will be silence on the other line. There is always silence on the other line after such a gaffe. Bob will curse himself. Of course—he's on the A-list. He's hot. He can pick up the phone and dial anybody—anybody who's in the club, that is—and it will be all right, no questions asked.

Until that wonderful day happens, though, Bob's dream is on hold. In the meantime, he must deal with small-time and small-minded editors who got *their* break years ago and clearly squandered it. They aren't the editors he envisioned would be at the helm of America's most prestigious publications. Is anyone, he wonders, motivated or able anymore to devote the time and attention needed to get the best out of him and his articles?

He recalls the classic essay, "Mistah Perkins—He Dead," by book editor Gerald Howard in *American Scholar* in 1989, which sums up for many the sorry state to which editing and publishing have declined today. Howard describes how, not that long ago, editors were more knowledgeable, more maternal, more passionate than their present-day counterparts. At the top of everyone's list—"a giant and a virtuoso of his craft"—was Maxwell Perkins, editor of F. Scott Fitzgerald, Ernest Hemingway, Ring Lardner, Thomas Wolfe and many others. Here's Howard's take on the passing, or dropping, of the literary torch since the Perkins era: "What used to be known as a gentlemen's profession has been transformed into a war of all against all. It is impossible to imagine that august figure Maxwell Perkins working happily or even successfully in this world, for his values—loyalty, honesty, taste, proportion, Olympian standards—are not always negotiable currency these days. . . . Editors of my generation and younger are resigned to and cynically humorous about the departure of a particular sort of grace from our world, intensely grateful when we encounter instances of it, and determined to emulate it to the extent that conditions will allow."

In other words, phooey on editors. Editors today are tremulous dabblers, Bob believes, forevering nit-picking or changing their skittish minds. One moment impossible to please, the next moment dispassionate, the next uncertain. Enthusiasm for the same piece ranges from: "I've never been so excited about an article" to just days later, "I don't know when it's going to run."

What would Bob like to see? He would like more editors to treat each query letter as if a living, breathing, human being belonged to it. He understands that lots of queries are poorly written and/or prepared, that they are plopped on an editor's desk in bundles and must be perused along with many others, and that the chore of wading through them is arduous. But if more editors would give each one at least more than a cursory glance and try to envision the person who sweated bullets to crunch it out—a writer who in all likelihood sat alone for many an evening fighting sleep, tedium, distractions, and enticements until he or she wrung that precise idea out of nothing, and then sent it to that particular editor's publication over hundreds of others—then Bob would sleep better knowing his queries were at least considered with care and not discarded like yesterday's E-mail.

Will that ever happen? Hah, pigs will fly first, thinks Bob, ever the realist. He figures amateurish, shoddy writers will never be in short supply, which means the quality of editors' slush piles will never improve, which means good queries (Bob's) will still be hard-pressed to stand out among the garbage. And to make matters worse, editors subconsciously want to keep it that way. That's right. A stack of poor queries, he suspects, actually makes an editor's job easier.

Say that again?

Here's how Bob sees it: If the vast majority of queries that editors receive were outstanding instead of junk mail, editors would have to devote a lot more time and concentration to them. It's like your "in" box at work. Most of what you get is stuff you can take action on swiftly, reroute, or trash. But every so often you get an unexpected report or memo from the boss that you silently groan about because you know you're going to have to study it in depth and reply to it. As Andy Rooney would say, "Don'tcha just hate that?"

Well, same goes for good query letters. Oh, editors complain about queries all the time, but deep down they *want* them to be as dull as dirt so they won't have to deal with them. It stands to reason, therefore, that when they *do* find a diamond query in the rough (Bob's), they're almost sorry, "Rats, now I have to run it through the channels, make a file, follow up, and stake my reputation on some writer I know nothing about." All of a sudden they've got a little query sister to babysit.

But there's also another, more diabolical and subconscious, reason why editors don't want to receive good query letters, muses Bob. Editors, with but a few exceptions, work primarily behind the scenes. Consequently, they rarely get much ink or glory. Their acclaim, when it comes, is mostly earned by developing an article that gets national attention, digging up a hot new writer on their own, or signing a big-name to an assignment. Kudos is rarely given to editors who "discover" beginners in their query stacks. (Uh, excuse me, didn't that writer find *you*?) Editors prefer to find them through their own initiative, not the writer's.

Where does that leave you and Bob? Somewhere between a paradox and a conundrum. To succeed, you must catch an editor's eye (which is good) but not let him know it (which is bad) via a query (which is bad) that doesn't look like one (which is good) that gets her attention (which is good) but not too much (which is bad) without being rejected (which is good).

Nobody said writing was easy, which is ironically why Bob still writes. If it wasn't so hard to break into writing, if his drive to see his byline in print wasn't so strong, and if his appetite for writing wasn't so ravenous, overcoming the grief involved in notching that first sale would be too high a price to pay for the accomplishment.

The only thing I would recommend to help ease Bob's and your efforts is to do what the pros do. First, avoid the slush pile by sending your letters to the right editor (more on this later). Second, play hard to get. Remember *Gone With the Wind*? Scarlett O'Hara's suitors literally fell over themselves trying to get her attention: "Marry me, Scarlett!" "Over here, Scarlett!" "Look at me, Scarlett!"—precisely what shouts at me between the lines of most slush-pile query letters.

But we all remember who won Scarlett's heart—cool, aloof Rhett Butler, that's who. He acted as if he were above it all and couldn't care less. He actually cared very much, but he knew he was superior to the others, knew she would see it, and let fate take its course. If she failed to see his qualities and interest, there were others who would. I can't tell you how often this subtle technique works and how often the theatrical method fails, but the ratio is probably ninety-five to five. So many queries are saturated with, "I really, really love your magazine and admire what you do and would consider it an honor if you would read this and if it appeared in your pages, blah-blah-blah" that when I see a query that introduces its idea and author cleanly and effortlessly, I do a double take. If you're in doubt, just imagine Paul Newman or Katharine Hepburn auditioning for a part (if anyone would have the nerve to ask them to). Professionals aren't pretentious.

And that's the dilemma. You want every editor to linger on your letter, *but not for the wrong reasons.* Bob needs to stand out from the herd—but through understatement, not overstatement. And that's a delicate and treacherous art. Good writers understand this intricate artistry and take years before they're proficient at it. Bob isn't there yet. But that's not his main concern. He wonders if, when he finally does master the craft of query writing, will there be any editors left who are sensitive and knowledgeable enough to know a good one when they see it? And that leads us, you guessed it, to my desk, the editor's.

From the Editor's Desk

Senior Editor Ann's day at her magazine office begins normally for her: hectic and swamped. On her desk are four colored folders that contain "blue lines" (final page proofs of the latest issue) that she must read ASAP. Two faxes are waiting for her at the switchboard—one from an agent with a copyright line on an excerpt Ann is reprinting that the copy department is screaming for; the other from a writer on assignment in London who's missed his connection to Rome for his interview with Gore Vidal and needs the author's phone number. In thirty minutes Ann has a phone interview lined up with a heart surgeon for her health column, and in an hour she's scheduled to conduct the planning meeting for the next issue, whose lead story was killed the previous day because the author missed the deadline, leaving the front of the book with a hole the size of a Buick. As she ponders all of this, the research department calls and says one of the "healthy" recipes in the cooking column actually contains more cholesterol than a crate of eggs, and legal follows up with the bad news that the only quotes that aren't total yawners by the celebrity profiled in the upcoming issue are not only potentially libelous but are garbled on the audiotapes, therefore cannot be verified, hence cannot be used.

At that moment, a thick folder filled with queries is placed on top of her teetering "in" box. The editor promised her she'd be off this detail by mid-year and the chore would be taken over by the new editorial assistant they were supposed to have gotten. But their final budget didn't allow for the new body so here she is, a highly paid, well-positioned, seven-year survivor in one of the most competitive, cutthroat industries in the world, still assigned to latrine duty. She picks up the folder and smacks it on top of the stack of query folders from the previous three weeks. "Out of sight, out of mind," she huffs.

As *Woman's Day* editor Geraldine Rhoades once said, "An editor can help a writer, but only God can help an editor."

But Ann, like many editors, is a former writer and remembers from whence she came. Giving in to her guilt and softheartedness, she opens one of the folders and skims through the first few letters. She sighs. The same tired ideas. The same passionless prose. The same sameness. She slams the folder closed—so much for compassion! Why can't writers see that they're insulting our intelligence—and theirs—with the stuff they send us? Why can't writers see what's best for our magazine? Why are so many writers allowed to ply their "craft" when they're obviously not suited for it or serious about it? She recalls a "wouldn't it be nice" conversation she once had with a fellow editor about organizing all magazines to require beginning writers to get a license proving they were serious about their career and had the necessary skills *before* they could canvas any publication.

But what really pains Ann isn't the query folder. It's knowing so many freelancers are out there, many who are trying and dreaming of breaking in—who have neither a chance of doing so nor a clue as to why. *And she can't do anything about it.* Ann loves her hectic, unpredictable, exhausting job—finding good writers and working with them to inform and astonish her readers in wonderful new ways is what she lives for, it's her dream come true—but one of her job's drawbacks is having to see firsthand so many other writers whose dreams will never come true.

Before Ann became an editor, she used to dream about how glamorous her career would be. She imagined herself chatting with writers like Toni Morrison and Tom Wolfe on her cellular phone on the way to work, schmoozing with literary agents and book publishers over long lunches at Italian bistro power tables, exchanging *bon mots* with best-selling authors who dropped by her office just to chat, and partying with the beautiful people when the sun went down.

Thankfully, she's now living part of that dream. Well, OK, so Norman Mailer's number may not be on her Rolodex, but last month her people (her assistant) took a meeting with Charles Grodin's people (his publicist); hey, it's a start. And all right, the only time she ever deals with agents and publishers is to hassle over outrageous contract demands over the phone, usually while wolfing down a brown-bag lunch—but hey, she gets great gossip on the Baldwin brothers. And so what if Bret Easton Ellis doesn't drop by her office occasionally for some latte and advice about his stalled career. Frankly, he gives her the creeps. As for hanging out with the beautiful people, though, that's one area where being an editor *does* pay off (in New York, no *real* party is complete without an editor).

So although Ann may not have reached the pinnacle of her career yet, she's definitely heading toward it on the fast track. That's why she has never once yearned to sit back, put her feet up, and devote an hour or two to the latest batch of slush-pile letters. Ann assumes, correctly, that any letter found in the slush pile must be from an amateur writer. (Pros know how to avoid that fate, which we'll get to in the next chapter.) It's not her business, or in her best interest, to deal with fledglings. That's the job of college professors, seminar instructors, English and journalism teachers. So since most editors don't expect to find anything worthwhile in the slush pile, they don't look very closely. And should, miracle of miracles, they do come across something intriguing, they may still discount it on the grounds that if something looks too good to be true, steer clear of it, "What's a nice writer like you doing in a place like this?"

Groucho Marx once said he wouldn't join any club that would accept him as a member. Ann feels the same way: She objects to working with any writer who would stoop to work with her (via the lowly slush pile). She, like most editors, got hooked on the good life (working with big-name writers) early on in her career. Once an editor discovers that neighborhood, she will never want to go back to the query-letter ghetto again. Shortly after getting "hooked," a sudden transformation occurs. The editor will start demanding that all queries look professional, are addressed to her personally, are right for her magazine, etc. Messily presented, lazily prepared, and/or poorly targeted query letters that she once tsk-tsked now launch her into ballistic tantrums.

Ann likes to tell writers: Visualize me as a bank-loan manager and yourself as a small-business loan applicant. If you want a loan from my bank, you'd better do your homework and put on a tie before you walk through my door because I'm not playing around. The slightest hint that you're not serious and you're gone. I could lose my job if too many of my loan applicants default. I am hired or not, promoted or not, fired or not based on the results I produce. So I need assurance that you're worth the money to invest in as a potential partner and are devoted to your business venture. I'm going to ask, "Who are you? Why are you doing this? Is this just a lark for you, or are you committed to the long haul?"

This, of course, begs the question: How can a writer convince an editor he's a professional and an experienced writer—when in reality he's just a beginner? And should he even try?

Editor Ann has no problem with beginning writers trying to pass themselves off as professionals because to do so successfully, they would have to do everything professionals do, which is what editors are always urging beginners to do! In fact, she admits, many writers have not only snookered her into thinking they were more experienced than they really were, but she even assigned major articles to them. Nothing pleases Ann more than to "discover" the next hot new literary phenom—amateur or professional. (Here comes the revelation . . . drum roll, please.) *No editor minds being "fooled" as long as the writer delivers the goods.*

Voila! That means you can get a major newspaper or magazine assignment, with no experience, from just a query letter. All Ann, or any editor, is looking for are neat, concise, well-structured, highly focused, well-written letters, and she knows beginners are just as capable of writing such correspondence as seasoned veterans. And that's the key word here: capable. Most any writer out there, Ann admits, is capable of these kinds of queries. They give the impression that you're thorough, knowledgeable, talented, and take pride in your work; in short, that you've been around the block. On the other hand, wordy, disorganized, inappropriate, poorly written, and/or sloppy query letters suggest your article will be likewise. Worse, they suggest you don't care about the impression you make and, consequently, aren't all that committed or motivated. As perennial best-selling job-search guru Richard Bolles (*The 1994 What Color Is Your Parachute?*) advises job-seekers: "The person who gets hired is not necessarily the one who can do that job best; but the one who knows the most about how to get hired."

Unfortunately, Ann doesn't usually get this kind of letter. What she gets mostly are form letters that have been clearly sent out to hundreds of publications simultaneously. In the job-search industry such letters are called "broadcast cover letters." They're popular with their senders because they involve lots of activity—you're constantly sending out new ones, tracking their progress, and getting back old ones—making you think you're accomplishing a lot. Motion equals momentum. Well, you may think you're a real writer by wallpapering your apartment with these reject letters, but the only person you're fooling is yourself (as evidenced by the number of guests who hum the *Twilight Zone* theme whenever they drop by).

In their book *Dynamite Cover Letters,* authors Ronald and Caryl Rae

Krannich write about this common but ill-fated, shotgun-style marketing method. Although their negative comments about the technique pertain to job seekers, the same also applies to freelance writers: "Like most direct-mail schemes engaged in by the uninitiated, this is the lazy person's way to riches. If you want to experience rejections, or need to fill your weekly depression quota, just broadcast several hundred résumés and letters to employers. Wait a few weeks and you will most likely get the depressing news—no one is positive about you and your résumé."

Just what a freelance writer needs more of: rejection and depression!

So there you have it. An up-close-and-personal look at what you and editors do, and most important, what each of us thinks of the other. I've tried my best to give an honest and in-depth profile of both sides, warts and all, without favoring one side over the other. My wish is that you've come away from this section with a greater understanding and empathy for editors—and a greater insight into yourself and where you want to go in your writing career. I know I've learned a lot about both editors and writers that I didn't realize before I sat down to write this chapter.

Perhaps the most significant thing I picked up was that there's no good guy or bad buy in this relationship. Even though each of us, editors and writers, may occasionally point fingers at one another, we know we couldn't exist or prosper without the other. And—come on, admit it—part of the reason we became an editor or a writer was the chance to one day work with a legend from the other desk. When I was a struggling writer, my dream was to sell something to Hugh Hefner or to know that Arnold Gingrich, and later Phillip Moffitt, of *Esquire* was actually reading my manuscript or query. As an editor, I'm now longing for the day when I pick up the phone and Dave Barry says, "John, I think I've finally written something funny enough for you to accept—I'M NOT MAKING THIS UP!!!"

I've been fortunate enough to have worked with a few legends, and each experience had a profound effect on the way I wrote or edited from then on. My hope is that someday—either through my daily course of business or through this book—I may affect a few other writers in the same positive and meaningful way. The better we all get, the better for all of us.

Questions & Answers

Q: What do editors *really* think of freelance writers?

A: Most of us see you as calculated risks. The two words that seem most apt in describing my feeling toward writers are "anticipation" and "anxiety." Each editor has his or her own criteria for choosing writers to assign, and the screening process is strict, ruthless, and painstaking. You would think, therefore, that when the writer's been selected, the assignment's been made, and the contract's been signed, the editor can finally sit back and sigh in relief.

Hardly. This is when an editor's the *most* nervous. Will the writer come through? Did I make the right decision in assigning him? Will this writer, whom I may have pitched to the editor-in-chief for weeks, live up to my hype or will he crash and burn—and if he does, will the boss ever trust my judgment again? For that matter, will I?

To give you an example of just how fretful editors can get, what do you think we do when a much-anticipated manuscript finally arrives? Chances are, we set it aside. For hours. For days. *We're afraid to look at it*. Why? Because we probably built up such expectation that we fear the writer will let us down. And surprisingly, the bigger the name, the *more* severe our anguish. That's because the more well-known you are or the longer you've worked with us, the more we expect from you—and the more apprehensive we'll be. So know this: Because you can make us and break us, you make us both desirous and nervous.

Q: Why don't editors give reasons why they reject queries? "It doesn't meet our present needs" tells me nothing. How can I persuade editors to explain why my queries are turned down?

A: You can't and editors won't. There are too many queries, too many reasons why each one fails, and too little time to explain the basics (which is where most queries break down). That's one of the painful realities of reading queries: I know *exactly* why I'm rejecting every one, but I don't have the time to communicate that to each writer in any quick, easy, or constructive way. Oh, I could jot down in the margins: "Sloppy presentation" or "Don't think you're right for it," or "Doesn't do anything for me." But such comments would probably just raise more questions. Trust me, I know. I've made such notes and gotten back furious letters from writers who misunderstood or argued with what I'd said. I also used to get such notes on my own queries, with the same result: What did she mean, "Your plot isn't compelling enough"? What isn't compelling about it?

Some well-intentioned editors try to help writers by sending back innovative reject letters featuring a checklist of reasons why the piece was rejected, with the appropriate boxes checked off. But these pose the same problem: How would a box marked "Characters not sufficiently developed" *really* help you?

Sometimes, though, a query or its writer will just barely miss. In these instances, if something about the writing, the idea, or the writer impresses the editor enough—and if she has a good heart for writers trying to break in—she may add a few comments or a short note. Encouragement never hurts, especially when it's warranted and has a chance of doing some good. If this is any solace, I don't know of any editor who does *not* do this from time to time.

Q: An editor once killed a manuscript he'd assigned to me, but I later sold it to one of his competitors. I've been sorely tempted to slip that fact into one of our subsequent conversations to needle, and educate, him. Should I?

A: No. A major writer once did that to me. Did it irk me? Just the opposite. It elated me. For two reasons. One, I'm always happy when a writer, especially one I've worked with, sells something. Writers have one of the toughest jobs in the world and deserve to get every break they can get. Second, it reaffirmed how good an editor I am—and how lame some of the supposedly "top" editors are at our competition.

What's worse, the comment didn't raise the writer's stature in my eyes, it lowered it. We editors are always looking over our shoulder at competing mastheads. All this writer's touché accomplished was to show me I have nothing to fear from my competitors if they're willing to stoop to buying such poorly done pieces.

Q: An editor at a magazine I've never approached before wants to assign my article, but she's offering a very low fee. I'm desperate to see my name in print, but I don't want to be taken advantage of. Is it proper to bargain? Will I brand myself an amateur by accepting her first offer? Could I blow it all by asking for more?

A: The magazine is probably offering you its bottom-level rate because you're new to it, but not because it's trying to screw you. I've never known a magazine to purposely and grossly underpay a writer just because it thinks the writer's naive and it can get away with it. Magazines are big businesses with huge accounting and administrative divisions that pay so many checks day in and day out that underpaying a writer here or there wouldn't make a speck of difference in the grand scheme of things.

When editors bend the payment rules, they almost always go the other way—by overpaying writers. Our magazine has certain payment rates; it can never pay below those rates but it can often pay above them—and many times does—if confronted by a demanding agent, a big-name client, or even a wolverine-jawed neophyte.

It is always wise to bargain. Accepting a magazine's first offer could indeed brand you as easy. Asking for more money, on the other hand, will make an editor think: "Be careful. This guy values his work and isn't playing games"—all things an editor *wants* to hear because they mean she's working with a professional. Remember, at this point in the negotiation process (when an editor wants to buy your piece), she needs you more than you need her. That may not be true from your end, but she doesn't know that.

What if the editor won't budge from the original offer? ("I'm sorry, but this is our rate for this department and we cannot go above it.") In that case, take it. She held fast, knowing you could tell her to take a hike. You can believe it was her final offer. But not all will have been lost. You at least tried and gained some respect in her eyes, which could pay off the next time you pitch her. In real estate the key word is location, location, location. In freelancing, it's byline, byline, byline. When you're starting out, always take a byline over a few more bucks.

CHAPTER THREE

The Article Query: The Ten Query Commandments

"My task which I am trying to achieve is by the power of the written word, to make you hear, to make you feel—it is, before all, to make you see. That—and no more, and it is everything."
Joseph Conrad

Now we get down to business: How to write the ideal magazine query letter. In my experience as a magazine editor, I have read my share of good and bad queries—more than twenty-five thousand of them and still counting. From what I've read, and from what my fellow editors have read, I can say without equivocation that few queries succeed, the vast majority fail, and both do so for one or more of the same reasons.

In this chapter you're going to learn the ten fundamentals that all queries must contain. For the purposes of this book, I will be strict. The reasons I'm so adamant are (1) it's not that much harder to write a letter that includes all ten basics than it is to write one containing none, and (2) if you do, you'll blow every other letter the editor gets that day out of the water. Trust me.

So, what are we waiting for? Let's get to the requisites.

The Ten Query Commandments

Each query letter must be, in order of appearance:

1. **Professional** (includes SASE, is error-free, is addressed to the right editor, etc.).

2. **New** (idea is fresh, set off, and up front).
3. **Provocative** (lead pulls you in).
4. **Creative** (presentation is offbeat).
5. **Focused** (story is narrowed down, length is kept to one page).
6. **Customized** (slanted to that magazine only).
7. **Multifaceted** (offers several options on how it could be done).
8. **Realistic** (instills confidence that you're reliable and the project's doable).
9. **Accredited** (includes your clips, credits, and qualifications).
10. **Conclusive** (confirms that you're the best and only writer to do it).

Professional

When you appear for a job interview, the interviewer is looking closely at a number of things besides your qualifications: your appearance, your behavior, your inquisitiveness, your preparation, etc. First impressions count heavily and can outweigh even the best of resumes. Same goes for query letters. Editors are looking for clear signs (as many as possible) that you have honed your skills and are ready to join the team, not someone who's just starting out and trying his hand at writing.

Editors are well aware of the fantasy that writing evokes, of the glamour of *being a writer*. It's a virus, like the flu, that seems to strike everybody at certain periods of their life. Unfortunately for editors, every day is that "certain period" in some writer-wannabe's life. We have to sift through the query stacks ourselves and weed out the obviously unsuitable-looking writers from the clearly professional-looking writers. Needless to say, the more professional your letter appears, the better chance you'll have of making the initial cut.

How can you make your letters look professional? When I receive a query, I look for ten signs that, if present, immediately qualify you for further consideration:
- Your letter is addressed to me (and if so, that I am the right editor)
- My name is spelled correctly
- My title is correct
- The magazine's name is spelled correctly
- The magazine's address is correct
- Your salutation is formal
- Your letterhead is simple and understated

- Your letter is neat and typed
- Your letter has been spell-checked
- You enclosed an SASE

Five of the first ten signs occur to the address block. Never underestimate this area. There's a lot going on here, a lot of places to falter. Let's start with the first one.

YOUR LETTER IS ADDRESSED TO ME AND I'M THE RIGHT EDITOR

The best way to avoid the slush-pile is to send your idea to the appropriate editor. Unfortunately, most writers inexplicably address their letters to whatever name is at the top of the masthead or, worse, to simply the "Editor," figuring their query will, at best, go directly to the top editor or, at worst, be eventually routed to the right person. Wrong squared. Instead of going to the top editor, these queries will go to the lowest editor (the slush-pile).

Slush-pile letters never reach your intended editor. They are packed in bundles and routed to editorial assistants who open them, remove the letters, rubber-band them together, and stuff them into a folder with all the other misaddressed queries that day. They are then divvied up to the newest or lowest-level editors on the staff who, believe me, dread reading them. Is that who you want passing judgment on your story idea that you've worked so long on? Or do you want it to arrive in the appropriate editor's "in" box by itself, personally addressed to the editor by name, tailored especially to that editor's subject area, and proposing precisely what he or she is looking for?

Whenever I get such letters (and I get very few), the writers have passed muster before I've even read a word. I feel I owe them a serious read because they have clearly expended more time and effort and thought than most of their peers.

This, of course, begs the question: How do I know which is the "correct" editor to send my query to? Here's what you do: Call the publication and ask for the editorial department. Ask the person who answers the phone this question: "Which editor handles [the specific topic you're querying about]?" If your query is health-related, for example, ask who the health editor is. If your idea is geared to a specific column or department, ask the name of that section's editor. Emphasize that you don't want to talk to this person; you just want his or her name so you can send something.

MY NAME AND TITLE ARE CORRECT

Next, confirm the spelling of that editor's name (don't assume simple names like "Karen" have only one spelling—I've seen this one, for instance, spelled Caren, Karyn, and Karenn). Don't assume either that the editor's title is correct (even if you're looking at the latest issue). Magazines are put to bed months before they hit the newsstands, and many changes (promotions, retirements, layoffs, transfers) can occur in the interim.

THE MAGAZINE'S NAME AND ADDRESS ARE CORRECT

It never hurts, while you have this person on the phone, to confirm the magazine's name and mailing address; publications change logos and locations again and again.

YOUR SALUTATION IS FORMAL

This is not the place to be cute or quirky; play it safe and conservative here with formal (Mr./Mrs./Ms.) greetings only. Sure, *Vibe* magazine may be hip and irreverent, but the senior editor you're addressing may not think your "Larry, dude!" greeting is so cool.

YOUR LETTERHEAD IS SIMPLE AND UNDERSTATED

Spare the theatrics here. That means no clip art clichés (typewriters, quills, fountain pens) running across the top of the page, no crayon colors, no fancy fonts, and no needless narcissism (Jim Smith, Writer). They reek of insecurity and amateurism.

YOUR LETTER IS NEAT, TYPED AND SPELL-CHECKED

A professional writer knows how to type and spell and uses a computer or typewriter. Although spelling every word correctly may not be as important to you as your idea or writing style, it is to most editors. Queries scrawled by hand or typed with strikeovers are signs that the writer hasn't written much. He's either just beginning or only dabbles with it as a hobby. Either way, he has grossly misunderstood the publishing industry.

YOU ENCLOSED AN SASE

Many writers don't include a self-addressed, stamped envelope with their queries. This is baffling. I can think of only two reasons why anyone would consider breaking this cardinal rule of freelancing, and both are poor excuses at best:

1. "I send out so many queries that I can't afford the added postage of an SASE with each one, too." Sorry, but that expenditure falls under "cost of doing business." A query is a business proposal, not a greeting card.

2. "Yeah, but a query's just a query; it's not the real deal. I don't object to attaching an SASE to a manuscript because by then you've asked for it or assigned it—it's worth the extra expense then. But if you think I'm going to pay twice for every pitch I make, you're nuts." Interesting logic. How do you expect to receive an answer to your query? Do you expect all the publications to which you send your unsolicited ideas to send your queries back on their dime? That's like you having to mail back—and pay for the envelopes, postage, and handling—all the junk mail you get every day. And do you know how much "junk mail" (slush pile queries) magazines get? As many queries as you send out, each magazine receives a thousand times more— and 95 percent of these are rejected. We would all go under if we had to pay the postage and handling on every one.

New

Do you do this? You read in your newspaper one day an article on, say, the large number of support groups forming across the country for parents accused wrongfully by their kids of child abuse. First time you've heard of it. "Gee," you say, "I should jump on that." So, hoping to catch the wave of the trend just as it's cresting, you send out a bunch of queries on that topic to major magazines.

Wipeout.

Why? Because you didn't add anything to the story. Once a new issue emerges and the news has broken, the story is already old. Anyone proposing the same general idea right afterward without any new spin or follow-up on it—no matter how hot the phenomenon may still be—will be hard-pressed to find a market. Try telling the same joke to someone who's still in stitches from hearing it moments before.

Rather than submit the same parents-support-group idea to all the appropriate magazines, think like those editors are thinking and try to alter the concept significantly enough to raise the stakes of the debate. Or focus on one key aspect of the issue (maybe just the therapists' angle—what's their story?). In short, put your own unique stamp on it, one that no one else has thought of, and you'll have a much better chance of landing a sale.

Editors have a neverending quest: They must continually keep their ears and eyes open to catch and tune into the next craze before anyone else does—or send up a trial balloon. If they don't get these fresh ideas from freelancers or their regular contributors, they have to do it themselves. A few years ago I attended a panel discussion in New York comprised of top magazine editors. One of the editors was from *Esquire*, and I told him about a catchy concept on a recent cover of his that had caught my eye. I asked him where that notion had come from (Had they done research through surveys or polls? Had they hired a high-priced consultant to foresee the future? Had they sent their editors and writers out into the field to dig up what America was really thinking about?). He simply grinned and said, "We made it up."

Moral of the story: Only so many editors abound, and we aren't any smarter than you. Don't wait for us to think up the next hot trend and then piggy-back on our idea. Set the new course yourself. Editors are constantly scouring the country for innovative, pioneer writers who can single-handedly alter the course of a debate all by themselves. Such writers are goldmines.

But coming up with a new concept is useless if you bury it in the sixth 'graph of your query. Many writers take forever to get to the point. Editors don't have time to wade through a page of introductory filler before they locate your article idea—they'll toss the letter before they get to it. So put the sucker right up front and flood it with klieg lights.

How should you do that? My executive editor recently instituted a new in-house policy among the editors that I now recommend to you: Any editor submitting an article idea to him must preface it with a head and subhead. "The instant I first see your idea," he told us, "I want to visualize how it would look in the magazine. If the head and deck don't grab me, neither will the concept—and that goes for the reader, too."

Place your head and subhead on a separate line right after your salutation. Center it and boldface it. And when you write the head and subhead, word it in whatever style (hip, sophisticated, convoluted, in-your-face) that magazine uses. If you haven't written many heads or subheads, don't just plunge in. Practice first; good heads are harder to write than they look. Check out your local newsstand and study the magazines' cover-line come-ons. You'll find that certain buzzwords or categories catch your eye more than others—and the more successful magazines drench their covers with them. Commit these pop motifs, and how they're worded, to memory. Then write your heads and subheads *exactly* like them.

Below are the most common and successful pitches. Under each one, I've listed some actual cover lines that I gleaned during one run-through of my local newsstand rack:

Numbers sell (the higher, the better)
"40 Tips to Get Organized"
"75 Ways to Stop Stress, Feel Great"
"100 New Ideas to Boost Your Child's Learning Power"

Superlatives sell
"Best-ever Keepsake Crafts"
"Say Cheesecake—America's #1 Dessert"
"America's Best Potluck Recipes"
"Crafts Spectacular"

"How-To's" sell
"How to Jump-Start Your Morning"
"Smart Strategies to Beat Allergies"
"Room-by-Room Clutter Busters"

Money sells
"Free Flower Stencil"
"Win a $500 House Cleanup"
"No-Cost Clothes"

Health and fitness sell (All the better if you
can combine health, fitness *and* money into one)
"Go on Our Money Diet—Spend Less, Save More"

Secrets sell
"M. Scott Peck's Secrets of Staying Young"
"Find Your Personal Secret to Diet Success"

Promises sell
"You *Can* Prevent Breast Cancer—Here's How"
"Thin Thighs in 30 Days"

Holiday issues sell
"Etiquette for the Holidays"
"68 Great Ideas for New Year's Eve"

Seasonal themes sell
"Summer Fiction Reading"
"Fall Fashion Guide"
"Winter Vacation Issue"

Questions sell
"Will Black Doctors Survive Health Reform?"
"Can California Chardonnays Really Compete
Against the Classic French Wines?"

Quizzes sell
"Are You a Hypochondriac? Take Our Test"
"The Great Compatability Quiz"

Truth sells
"Why Women Crave Candy"
"How We Become What We Are"

Myths sell
"The Sex-Bias Myth in Health Care"

Provocative

I love leads. I also love one-liners, ad libs, movie catchphrases, billboard blurbs, movie print-ad teasers—anything short and punchy. Compression is power and powerful compression is genius. Here are some of my favorites:

> Let's begin at the end: A boom looms in tombs.
>> (*Thomas R. King writing about how society is catering to the maturing baby-boom generation,* Wall Street Journal, *June 23, 1989.*)

> Richard Nixon advising George Bush on handling the media is like Quasimodo giving advice on grooming and personal hygiene.
>> (Los Angeles Times *columnist Howard Rosenberg's reaction to Richard Nixon acting as a media consultant to then-President Bush, January 18, 1989.*)

> Some strokes past midnight, the dank Hudson River air is heating up in explosive puffs outside the Shelter, a dance club in Lower

Manhattan. The doorman is facing down a tiny Latino woman with a mouth wider than the Lincoln Tunnel. "What? I say WHUT is your PROBLEM, Mis-tuh Larger Than Life?"

(Gerri Hirshey profiling actress Rosie Perez in GQ, *August 1992).*

Bottom of the third, bases jammed, two outs, and the guy with the artificial hip was up.

The pitcher told the left fielder to move in. Mind your own damn business, the outfielder replied.

So the pitcher felt a bit spiteful. "Go ahead and drop it in front of him," he told the batter, and then he lobbed the next pitch slow and without spin, about waist high, fat as a pumpkin.

Al Freyberger hit it square. The ball arced toward the sun, lolled high among the sea gulls, then came down where no glove could reach it. It skipped along the bumpy grass toward the fence, and three runs scored.

Gosh, he walloped it. Old Al's face lit up as he chugged into second. He stomped some dust out of the base while he caught his wind. It would have been a home run sure thing, back when Al still had good wheels, before the hip implant, before he turned 83.

(Barry Bearak observing a Florida senior slow-pitch softball league, Los Angeles Times, *December 18, 1985).*

Peter Jacobi, the best editing/writing instructor I ever had and currently a professor at the Indiana University School of Journalism and a speaker/consultant for Folio (a series of regional conferences for magazine professionals), is another aficionado of great leads. Article leads do a lot, he often tells his classes. They establish your subject. They set the tone. They attract attention. And they guide the reader into your story. Query leads, like their article counterparts, accomplish the same things.

The goal of a lead is to stun the reader and pull him into the text, which is against most editors' nature. Reading queries is tedious. The last thing an impatient, overworked, bored editor wants to do is read every query letter from beginning to end. She's skimming each one for any excuse to bolt. Your job—your lead's job—is to show her as fast as you can that *your* letter is different.

I realize this is a lot of pressure to put on your first 'graph. But there's a lot riding on any first impression. A strong lead is your job-interview handshake, your supermarket pick-up line, your cold-call phone solicitation, your first meeting with the in-laws. The fate of most queries is decided in the time it took you to read this sentence. That's it, and you're history. Your lead must resemble a Joe Louis left hook: short—and with all your weight behind it.

One way to learn how to write great leads is to periodically spend an afternoon at your local library or newsstand and skim the magazine racks. Study nothing but the leads of the articles inside. Then imagine each piece is not an article, but a query letter, and you're the editor deciding their fate. Which ones would you read further? Which ones would you pass on? Eventually, patterns will emerge that, after time, will become second-nature to you: This approach usually works better than that one, that style is better suited for this kind of story. You will discover that there are not just a handful of different lead styles, but dozens. And most important, you will find the method *you* prefer. Hone that to perfection, and your queries will always be read. From beginning to end.

Creative

Sometimes it's OK to be quirky and offbeat in a query letter—within reason (which I'll get to in a minute). The reason you want to be different is, well, to be different. Most query letters look the same. If I'm reading a batch of thirty, they all begin to look like one generic letterhead after a while. If your letter, however, jars my concentration—even a little—then you've accomplished something none of the other twenty-nine queries have. It's just an edge, but an edge nevertheless.

Here are two easy ways to stand out: (1) with your layout, and/or (2) with your writing style.

Anything that physically alters the standard letter format is a blessing. You can do this several ways: by inserting boldface, italic or underlined subheads throughout the text; by indenting or justifying paragraph blocks; by bulleting or numbering paragraphs; by adding charts or boxes; by including a P.S. at the end. If you use a computer, play around with its desktop publishing capabilities to give your queries some pizzazz.

Just don't overdo it. Quirky and offbeat does *not* mean going hog-wild with bizarre fonts, giant type, garish stationery, caps and exclamation points everywhere. The most unusual query I ever received was designed in the form of a four-page foldout greeting card. Each of the four pages featured individual clip art, shaded heads, colored type, checkerboard borders, poems, cartoons, different fonts. I felt really bad because, even though the writer had done an awful lot of work designing it and customizing it to me person-ally (even the poem was written for and about me!), I couldn't assign the the article to the writer—even if his idea had intrigued me (which it didn't). I treasure originality, but this query was so flamboyant that it made me leery of the writer. Who knows what you'd get back?

You can also stand out by going out on a limb stylistically. I got my first editing job doing that. After getting no response to several of my standard, conservative, "Per your advertisement in last Sunday's newspaper, I am applying for the position of. . . ." letters, I said to heck with it and sent a wild, off-the-wall stand-up routine on me and my qualifications to the next ad for an editorial position I saw. I had nothing to lose. I figured the editor had a sense of humor or he didn't. He did. He called and asked me to come in. In the interview he said he'd never gotten a letter like that before and wanted to meet me "just to see what kind of person would send in such a crazy letter." I got the job.

Since that time I've had writers query me who, after reading articles of mine or seeing me speak and sensing we were on the same wavelength, sent me letters that really stretched the boundaries. I loved 'em! Lucky for them, I admire risk-taking and understand how crucial it is for beginning writers to get noticed. I'm a writer, too, and I know what it feels like to get the twenty-second rejection on a great idea and wonder what else can you do. So don't ever be afraid to try something different—as long as your query also contains the other nine things I'm recommending in this chapter.

Focused

If one of your queries has been getting nowhere, maybe your idea is too broad. Maybe you're confusing an angle with a subject. To you, an idea worded in broad-brush fashion (health-care reform) may seem legitimate because it presents your concept on a large canvas. But to an editor, such murals are too vast to comprehend. What's the story? In your creative pro-cess, make the big ideas your starting points, never the endpoint.

Editors want concepts narrowed down to their lowest common denomi-nator. Let's take the idea above, "health-care reform." Start by zooming into its middle—or out to its fringe areas. You'll dig up subtopics such as health-care benefits, health-care costs, health-care access, longterm care, health-care insurance, etc. But these ideas are still too broad for an editor to work with. OK, then slice off one of these that appeals to you. Let's say you select "health-care benefits." Burrow into that and look for interesting nooks and crannies. When you find a niche, see if there's one inside that. Keep slicing, keep focusing, keep narrowing until you can't go any farther. In the end you should arrive at something like "Ten Health-Care Reform Benefits Minority Business Owners Will Never Get." Now *that's* a story. Not only that, it will be your story alone because nobody else will send it in—none of your competitors will have expended the effort you did.

Here are three other hypothetical query ideas. In each case I've started with a typical broad concept, then progressively narrowed it down in two subsequent renditions to a more editor-friendly variation—with the latter being the most desirable. Which query version would you choose if you were an editor?

An ex-GI returns to Vietnam to seek answers to what happened there.

An ex-GI returns to South Vietnam to tour his former battle-field, wander among the ghosts, and purge his soul.

An ex-GI returns to Chu Lai, Vietnam, to tour his former battlefield, thank the family who saved his life, and apologize to the survivors of the family he killed.

Drugs in America—what can be done?

Drugs in America—it's not up to the government to solve the problem, it's up to the communities.

Drugs in America—How one Hartford, Illinois, community cut gang presence on their streets by 85 percent by using an innovative system of patrols, surveillance, and communication to expose gang activities.

Sleep disorders among the elderly.

The big three sleep disorders among the elderly—insomnia, sleep apnea, and restless legs syndrome.

A photo essay of an elderly woman with restless legs syndrome as she's tested during one night with the newest experimental-drug treatment.

Customized

The most egregious mistake an editor can make is to propose an idea to his own editor-in-chief that is clearly wrong for his publication. In the cutthroat publishing world of New York, that would be a no-brainer career-ender. Editors are supposed to know their own publication, backwards and forwards, from the subtle nuances of its To Your Health department to the peculiar plastic-surgery questions that always titillate the editor-in-chief in celebrity profiles. That's why most article ideas come from editors, not freelance writers: They know their product and customers best. So how are you supposed to pique the interest of a publication whose particular wants and needs are unavailable to you?

By joining the staff.

I don't mean literally; the commute alone would kill you. I mean unofficially, by acting as one of the publication's roving editors. Any writer is, in effect, a field editor for the publications he sells to. Impossible, you say? Didn't you just say such information is unobtainable and confidential? Yes. Then how can we know more than your magazine's own editorial staff?

Pick up any newsstand magazine and flip to the masthead where the staff is listed. You will most likely see a heading called "Contributing Editors." These are freelance writers like yourself, not staff members. They have been given this exalted title because they've demonstrated, through studying the magazine in depth and previous assignments for the magazine, that they understand the publication and its readers very well. In fact, they're so in sync with the editorial direction that they often know what the editors want before the editors do.

In addition to contributing editors, each magazine also calls on dozens of other "regulars" whom they know they can call on in a pinch to knock something out, or whose queries are always welcomed because they're consistently about things the editors would want. (And when their ideas draw a blank, they know the magazine and its staff so well that, more often than not, they can convince the editor she's wrong and they're right.) Editors dream about such writers.

But we already know how to study a magazine, you counter. Hmm, do you really? If you're thoroughly researching every magazine you pitch, then how come your queries keep coming back? There's a right and a wrong way to study a magazine. The wrong way is to peruse *Writer's Market* and shotgun a bunch of queries to all the publications that buy the kind of article you have in mind. The right way is to follow this foolproof five-point procedure:

1. Peruse *Writer's Market* and list all the magazines that buy the kind of article you want to write.

2. From that list, select six magazines.

3. Obtain the six *most recent* issues of those publications from your local library (that's a total of thirty-six magazines: six issues of six different magazines).

4. Separate one magazine's six issues from the pile. Pore over the issues from cover to cover—its features, its departments, its design, its ads, its letters-to-the-editor, its cartoons, etc. Analyze one category completely before you go to the next (i.e., look at all six issues' articles first, then all their ads, all their letters, etc.). Study all six until you could practically compose the magazine's mission statement. Look for these along the way:

   • Study the magazine's ads, but pay particular attention to the smaller ones (a condom ad says more about its readers than a Ford ad).

   • Leaf through recent *Advertising Age* and *Adweek* magazines for the magazines' ads to its own industry; these will show you who it's really targeting.

   • Who writes for the magazine? Are its writers experts? locals? staffers? freelancers? top names?

   • Look at its covers and cover lines. Would your article fit in or look out of place there?

   • How are the articles' heads, decks, and callouts written? ("Heads" are the titles. "Decks" are the subtitles that run below the titles and sum up the article in an intriguing fashion. "Callouts" are brief sound-bite excerpts that are lifted from the text and showcased on subsequent pages to either lure readers back into an article they may have left or to draw readers into an article they may have skipped.) Are they highbrow, tantalizing, plain, satirical, cute, corny? If there's a consistent style and tone to them, mimic that in your query.

   • Read the editor's column. You won't get a clearer message than this. Here the editor's talking to you about what's important to him and his readers.

   • Most magazines and newspapers feature regular columns (money, health, consumer, movie and book reviews, etc.). Although you won't be able to supplant writers whose bylines regularly grace these departments, the sections are worth studying because their topics are often microcosms of the big picture; i.e., a tiny column item on hot new CD-ROM discs could mean a lengthy feature article on new advances in home computers could also work.

5. Repeat the procedure for the other magazines.

My method is hard and tedious, no question. But that's the beauty of it. Because it involves so much research, most writers skip it, which is why most writers are still dreaming of bylines. Therefore, the field's wide open to *you*, if you're willing to do the extra work. The handful of writers who sell, and sell regularly, to major magazines and newspapers research their markets thoroughly before they even think about composing a query. The query letter is the last stage of the process for them, not the first. To approach a magazine without knowing what it buys and doesn't buy, what its personality or writing style is, who its readers are, what it's done and what it needs, would be inconceivable to a seasoned pro.

I've long marveled at the amount of work professional writers put into their preliminary research and pitches—without any guarantee beforehand that their work will pay off—but I've also long envied the ease with which they sell those ideas to us and other magazines. Their work ethic is in stark contrast to what I see from most beginning writers. I once likened the role of beginning freelancers trying to sell an article to a publication to that of a band of serfs trying to scale an enemy's castle walls. The task seemed not only formidable but impossible, especially after we were beaten back time after time. When I was hired as an editor, though, and assumed the role of defending the castle, I soon realized how easy it was to circumvent our defenses—especially if a well-trained army of knights attempted it. Those professionals prepared themselves more, knew which tools to use and how to use them, and knew precisely which of our soft spots to probe. We were no match for such veterans; they were up and over our walls in no time.

Multifaceted

Always give an editor more than one reason to say yes. Suggest more than one place in the magazine for it, more than one way to do it, more than one thing to peg it to and more than one element to accompany it. This way, you'll combine several queries into one with each submittal. Here's how:

In the preceding commandment you learned how to target your article idea to the right magazines. Here's where that knowledge pays off. After presenting your notion, suggest to the editor more than one place for more than one way to write it. Write something like: "If you don't see my idea working as a feature article, perhaps it could fit better, with some alterations, as a Money department item, as a short Q&A in the People column or as a quiz for your Back Page feature." Never assume the editor will automatically think of such spinoffs.

Next, put yourself in the editor's place and figure out when your article might best run. This is always a priority with editors. We're always asking: Is this idea old news? Is this the ideal time for it? Is this too premature for the season? See if it could tie in with an upcoming event or time of year. Scan the calendar for the next two years and see if your article fits into any slot, no matter how far-fetched. You'd be surprised at how often it will (fiftieth anniversary of the end of World War II? Father's Day? Oscar ceremony? Christmas? Election year? Summer? Upcoming movie/record/ book?).

And finally, always sweeten the pot. In case the editor is still undecided, mention what other elements you intend to include with the piece. Photos? A sidebar? Charts and graphs? A resource box for where to write/call for more information? Editors love extras. The more you make them think they're getting a freebie with the deal, the better your odds.

Realistic

I once received a query letter for an essay about "how our universe, our planet, and humankind unfolded through time, our mistakes, our achievements, and our hope for a meaningful future." Just *some* of the topics to be discussed were "the origin and nature of the universe, human origins, prehistory, the first civilization, the Renaissance, human problems of the twentieth century, and a code of ethics for the twenty-first century."

Needless to say, I didn't ask to see it. Maybe I should have. Maybe we would have found the answers to life's most vexing questions and could have all gone home. But I didn't. I suspected the project might be just a bit more complicated than the writer realized.

The problem with queries like this is, not only is the article undoable, but the writer doesn't know it's undoable. An editor must trust you completely. There must be no doubt that the assignment can be completed and that you can do it. Whether you're asking an editor to send you to Patagonia to witness the solar eclipse, to Wall Street to forecast the stock market, or to your garage to scrounge for collectibles, you'd better know what you're getting yourself into. The only thing worse than an editor saying "No" to your query is an editor saying "Yes"—and you realizing you can't pull it off.

I committed this cardinal sin several years ago. I was taking a comedy-writing class. One of the guest speakers was a writer for the *Tonight Show*. We were in stitches from the moment the guy walked into the room. He was so funny and spontaneous, I thought he was a natural for a Q&A. I sent a query about him to an inflight magazine. The editor, whom I'd never approached before, liked the idea so much he called me to say he had slotted my piece for his next cover! Unfortunately, I had never thought to ask the writer beforehand if he was available (he wasn't), if he would do it (he wouldn't), or if the show even allowed its staffers to talk to the press (it rarely did during the Johnny Carson era, and when it did, it *never* allowed them to talk about Johnny, which was what the editor wanted most). Not only did I kill my own assignment but I destroyed any hope that that editor would trust me again. I was so ashamed I never queried him again.

What sort of query gaffes can destroy your credibility?

- Proposing a major investigative report—in 1,500 words. This tells an editor you've never done a project of this kind. A "major investigative report" requires between 5,000 and 10,000 words.

- Proposing an exclusive interview with Princess Di—in two weeks. You're dreaming, right? This tips off an editor that you're a novice at interviewing major personalities. Getting an exclusive with someone of this magnitude would take a seasoned pro months, if not years, just to arrange, let alone interview, edit, and write.

- Proposing a Christmas magazine story—in September. This shows an editor you're ignorant about lead times (and you thought you were brilliant approaching him so far in advance!). Magazines send their December issues *to the printer* about that time. They start planning their December issues at least a year in advance, maybe more.

- Proposing an article—that you've already written. This signals two things to an editor: (1) Your piece has probably been rejected elsewhere, and if so, it has one strike against it; or, (2) if it's original, then your piece has just struck out. Never write an article from scratch (unless it's humor, fiction, or an essay, in which case it's OK) or send it in unsolicited without discussing it with an editor first. The reason is that the odds of you having conceived—without any editorial input beforehand—the precise topic, angle, sources, structure, style and length the editor would have wanted is about a million-to-one. The vast majority (90 percent) of articles I assign undergo major restructuring. Few finished products resemble their writer's original query blueprint. Editors often have to put their own or their editor's or their publisher's spin on a story—not for spite or ego (OK, sometimes) but usually because of situations beyond our control (the magazine's guidelines, what the magazine's done before, what the magazine needs to beef up or curtail, etc.).

Accredited

The crucial element in your query is where you describe yourself. (Huh? Editors don't care about me, you say. They're only interested in the bottom line: my story.)

We're interested in what you've got, sure, but not as much as who you are. I don't see many editors run down the hall shouting, "My God, start engraving the Pulitzer, you won't believe what this guy proposed!" But I have seen editors swoon at the possibility of inking a particularly hot new writer they discovered. I would feel much more confident giving a great writer a mediocre topic than giving a mediocre writer a great concept. (If you haven't sold anything yet, don't fret, there's a way around that, which I'll address in a minute.)

So, if you take away only one thing from this book, make it this: Editors are never buying just the idea; they're buying the writer *and* the idea—in that order.

How do you sell yourself in your query? There are three ways: (1) Tell us what you do, (2) tell us what you've written and, (3) show us what you've written.

TELL US WHAT YOU DO

Your query is like a sales presentation. The best salespeople are those who know how to "qualify" their buyers (in this case, the editor). That means knowing the key motivators that will sell the editor on you—and pushing those hot buttons often. Therefore, if you have any knowledge about, experience in, or qualifications relating to your query idea, tell us about them. A piece on auto-repair scams may be appealing, but if you once worked as an auto mechanic and know what goes on behind closed hoods, the idea's not only appealing it's a sure sale.

An editor once said, "Too many writers hold aces, but they just don't play them the way they should." That's why being humble is deft on a first date, death on a first query letter. Don't worry about how it'll look or if you're overdoing it. The competition for your article slot is *huge*. This is your fifteen-second read-through in front of the director, kid. The line of candidates stretches around the building. The producer's looking at his watch. *You have very little time.*

Make sure, however, that whatever you say is related to your idea. Eliminate everything else. Going on endlessly about your entire background, most of which won't have anything to do with your query, is a common mistake that has killed many submissions.

This example, from a query from freelancer Larry Richardson, illustrates how to indicate a special ability to write about a unique subject:

> I am a freelance health reporter who writes and edits newsletters for physicians. With your permission, I would like to use my "inside" information, anecdotes, surveys, and experts to write an article called, "Dr. Kevorkian Doesn't Walk Alone in the Shadow of Death." For this article, I will recount an actual instance of physician-assisted suicide involving a doctor.

In short, make the difference between you and your competition so vast, indisputable and unfair that you give an editor no alternative. If you err at all in this task, err by including too much, never too little.

TELL US WHAT YOU'VE WRITTEN

Don't throw in everything you've done; we don't want a resume. Just a quick overview of where you've published and the type of work it was (if you've sold articles or books similar to your query topic, be sure to highlight it). For example, if you're proposing to interview Clint Eastwood, it's imperative for editors to know if you've done celebrity interviews before. We want to know where you are in your career. The farther along, the better your chances.

Which brings us to the old bugaboo: What if you haven't sold anything, not much, or only to small or regional publications? Don't say anything. No editor will know, or even assume, that your failure to list any credits means you haven't sold anything. It simply looks like you chose not to mention them. What *will* kill your letter is if you panic and blurt out the truth. *Never* volunteer that you haven't sold anything or give even a hint that you're a beginner. The only exception is if you're querying a minor or regional publication, it's OK to say you've sold to small markets before.

Here's an excellent example from a query about Route 89 from freelancer Dan Baum. Notice how he only highlights qualifications that match his topic; all other background information has been omitted:

> I now cover the northern Rockies on a freelance basis for the *Los Angeles Times, Chicago Tribune, Philadelphia Inquirer, Newsday, San Francisco Examiner*, and others. I also write for *Outside, Sierra, Buzzworm*, and *Pacific Northwest* magazines, and just finished a five thousand-word piece for *Smithsonian* about the fall and rise of Butte, Montana.

SHOW US WHAT YOU'VE WRITTEN

We need to analyze your writing style, so let us also see a couple of clips (preferably ones similar in tone and subject matter to your query). Here we can spot the consistencies in your style, study your thoroughness, look at your structure, etc. (*Important*: If you can, include only articles that editors hardly touched and assignments in which you really hit it off with editors. That's because savvy editors, knowing clips can be unreliable, sometimes track down the ones who edited them and ask how much work was done on them and how easy you were to work with. In *Get Published!* authors Diane Gage and Marcia Hibsch Coppess quote Kate White of *Mademoiselle* as observing half-jokingly, "A couple of editor friends and I occasionally threaten to start a computerized Universal Product Code that would appear at the end of every article to indicate to other editors how much the writer had been edited.") As with your credits, don't enclose reprints from small or regional publications unless you're querying the same type of publication.

Conclusive

Everybody knows what it's like to deal with a slothful salesclerk, a sluggish secretary, or an aloof attendant. One of your priorities, therefore, should be to convince the editor that you're alert, prepared, and passionate. Experienced editors have a good nose for reading between the lines of query letters. We can tell if you're just mass-marketing your idea for cash or if you really care about your project and our publication. Are you knocking on any old door, or did you knock at mine, at only mine, and for a reason? The last thing we want to read is an indifferent letter that's just going through the motions. As Gertrude Stein said, "There's no there there."

So how do you show an editor that you care about your proposal and that you've got the goods to deliver it? Enthusiasm. If you have it, it jumps off the page; if you don't, the page just lies there. See if these examples help:

The Wrong Way

Playwright Ossie Davis is a person I would like to profile for your magazine. You saw him in *Jungle Fever* and *Do the Right Thing*. He's seventy-eight and still going strong. A great role model, activist, and inspiration to your readers.

The Right Way

Ossie Davis crossed the stage with slow, mannered steps, peered solemnly around the great hall, gripped the lectern like he was going to hurl it into the audience, and then spoke in a voice that seemed to emanate from some deep sepulchral chamber. I thought I'd heard the voice of God himself.

The American Academy of Motion Picture Arts & Sciences will honor Davis later this year for his vast achievements as an artist and activist. To preview and commemorate that occasion, I would like to profile Davis and give your readers a taste of the power, eloquence, and nobility I experienced on that memorable day. . . .

An editor asks, which writer wants this assignment more? Which one is better prepared? Which one is more knowledgeable? Which one is more inspired by the topic? My longtime advice to writers: Show me you care and show me what you've got. Even if you get shot down, go down in flames.

Those are the Ten Query Commandments. Follow them—or face the consequences. To show you how all ten principles would look together in one query letter, I created an ideal query letter on the next few pages that you can refer to as a checklist whenever you're composing a new query.

Ideal Article Query Letter

1.

Jane Smyth
World Report Editor
Travelcade Magazine
123 Main Street
New York, NY 12345
Dear Ms. Smyth:

2.

Story proposal
"Rio—sunny, sexy . . . and on the skids?"

3. & 4.

Postcard from Rio de Janeiro, 1996: *It's everything you said it would be, Marge. Carnaval brings out the masses all right, the water's green and glowing, and the girl from Ipanema still goes walking. The difference is, the only masses I saw at Carnaval were tourists, the only reason the water's green and glowing is because it's polluted, and the girl from Ipanema goes walking all right— but only with a bodyguard. I think grand ol' Rio's gone the Beirut route, Marge.*

P.S. But I still had a great time—with a few tips I picked up.

5.

Once one of the premiere locales of the globe—its very name conjuring up passionate, pulsating images—Rio de Janeiro has for the last few years degenerated into a shabby third-world cesspool of crime, pollution, corruption, and decrepitude. My article will explain why *o marviloso cidade* has fallen so low and how, with the help of an innovative and resourceful tourism campaign, it's finally begun to turn itself around. I'll show your readers how they can now enjoy its charms while avoiding the sore spots.

1. PROFESSIONAL

This writer confirmed by phone which editor he should send his query to. He asked the "Editorial" department which editor handles the topic (travel) he was querying about. Then he confirmed the editor's name (by asking the person on the phone to spell it, he discovered an odd spelling that saved embarrassment), title, and mailing address. With one thirty-second phone call, he avoided the slush-pile.

2. NEW

The writer's job is not to give an editor a lazy, worn-out, standard idea. This subject is not only relevant and interesting to this magazine's readership but as unexpected a story about Rio as you'll ever read. In addition, the writer put the idea up front and separated it from the body of the text so the reader saw it first. Then he set it off again with a boldface, centered headline.

3. & 4. PROVOCATIVE AND CREATIVE

It never hurts—and usually helps—to be a little different. This writer designed his lead as a clever postcard, which tied into the theme of the piece nicely.

5. FOCUSED

The best ideas are those narrowed down to one aspect of a general topic. Rio's sexy, sunny reputation is a stereotype. So this writer took a magnifying glass to that image and searched until he came up with a new twist.

6.

My article will fit nicely into the *World Report* section of your magazine, which investigates travel-related trends in different regions of the world. Accompanying the piece is a sidebar on "Where It's Safe to Go, Where It's Not" and a map/chart of the city showing the nature of crimes committed against tourists over the past five years, where they've occurred the most and the least and how much they've increased.

7.

Other options would be to:
• Interview Fernando da Silva, Rio's outspoken chief of police for your People Spotlight department. Silva tells it like it is and shows tourists exactly what to do and what not to do when exploring Rio. (When he was profiled on PBS last year, the station got more than five thousand letters and calls!)
• A checklist for your Top Ten department: "Rio's 5 Safest Beaches—and 5 Worst."
• A how-to for your Travel Smart column: "How Not to Look Like a Tourist in Rio."
• A quiz for your Games page: "What Would You Do?" (Readers will be confronted with actual mugging situations that have victimized tourists and given multiple-choice options on how they would react.)

6. CUSTOMIZED

Any letter targeting a particular section of a magazine will grab an editor's attention because such a thing happens as often as a solar eclipse. This writer aimed his article for the magazine's World Report section, enabling the editor to visualize how and where it could best fit into the mix.

7. MULTIFACETED

Always give an editor more than one reason to say yes. This writer presented more than one place in the magazine for his idea, more than one way to do it, and more than one element to accompany it. This way, he actually combined several queries into one.

8.

> For your information, I have access to more than a dozen experts and travel authorities here and in Rio de Janeiro. Depending on which option you prefer, I could deliver a 3,000-word World Report, a 1,000-word People Spotlight profile, or a 500-word Top Ten checklist, Travel Smart column, or Games page quiz within two months of assignment.

9.

> As for my credentials, I have visited Rio more than a dozen times during the last ten years as *National Geographic*'s South America correspondent and once worked for the U.S. Embassy there handling tourist affairs. I have also served as a travel consultant for Hyatt and Marriott hotels in both Rio and Buenos Aires, where I regularly lectured to visitors about crime and safety. My book, *Carnaval—Samba and Soul*, had its twelfth printing last year.

10.

> Rio is one of tourism's perennial landmarks and cash cows. Its decline, and subsequent rise from the ashes, is a lesson other glamour capitals that have sunk into disrepute should heed—are you listening New Orleans, Acapulco, Miami? The article can also alert future travelers to and prepare them for what may become an unfortunate and recurring pathology among the world's great cities during the next millennium. As you can see from this letter, I can tell this story from several unique and exclusive perspectives, any one of which would be important and fascinating for your readers. The story needs to be told, Ms. Smyth, and told now; let me be the one to alert your readers.

8. REALISTIC

An editor wants to know one thing: Is the piece doable and can you pull it off? This writer measured how long each section of the magazine usually runs, outlined the sources he would use, and estimated a reasonable time frame to bring in the complicated project.

9. ACCREDITED

Editors want to know how qualified you are to do the piece. This writer left no doubt, listing the skills he possessed and special knowledge he'd gained, and attached clips (similar in style and content to the proposed article) of previous work.

10. CONCLUSIVE

This is your moment to convince the editor, beyond a shadow of a doubt, that you are the most qualified, the most prepared, the most experienced, the most logical, and the most passionate writer to do the piece. This writer's enthusiasm comes through; he didn't give the editor a chance to say no.

1.

Enclosed are reprints of some of my previous articles. If you would like to discuss any of these ideas further, please call my office at the number below. Thank you very much for your consideration.

Sincerely,

John Jones
123 Maple Drive
Anytown, CA 90000
213-555-9000

Enclosures:
Clips
SASE

Sample Letters

Dear Mr. Wood:

I am a freelance health reporter who writes and edits newsletters for physicians. With your permission, I would like to use my "inside" information, anecdotes, surveys, and experts to write an article for *Modern Maturity* readers called "Dr. Kevorkian Doesn't Walk Alone in the Shadow of Death."

Reading the popular media, you'd assume that Jack Kevorkian is the only physician helping terminally ill patients take their lives. But that impression is far from the truth. The AMA's governing body recently reaffirmed its opposition to physician-assisted suicide, but there was strong dissent. Illinois delegate Ulrich Danckers, MD, complained that the AMA position "fails to respond to the crying need of our patients in prolonged agony." And University of Arizona bioethics professor Kennneth Iserson, MD, said he was amazed at the number of primary-care doctors he surveyed who admitted assisting in suicides. In fact, 89 percent of the doctors and nurses surveyed by the *American Journal of Public Health* agreed that it is sometimes appropriate to give medication to ease suffering, even if it may hasten death.

The prevalence of assisted suicide is in line with public sentiment. In 1992, the *Journal of the American Medical Association* published a poll that found that 64 percent believe doctors should be allowed to assist in a terminally ill patient's suicide.

For this article, I will recount an actual instance of physician-assisted suicide involving a doctor other than Dr. Kevorkian and place the story in context with the larger ethical questions. Experts on both sides will be interviewed.

Please let me know at your earliest convenience if you are interested in this article. Thank you.

Sincerely Yours:

Larry Richardson

COMMENTS

Sounds like a potential hard-hitting health piece, and its angle is unique and timely. Provides a lot of data in a little space. I passed this to our health editor, who liked it and presented it to the executive editor.

Dear Mr. Wood:

Pets spark up our lives. The kitty runs after a ball of yarn and purrs sleepily as it curls into a lap. The dog barks happily when we come home, always ready to lick a hand and offer a head to pat. The human-animal bond plays an important part in so many peoples' lives, from the four-year-old learning to feed and care for a soft, furry pup, to the graduate landing a job far from home who gets a gray tabby to share her apartment, to the retired couple who enjoy frolicking in the park with their Irish setter. Erwin Small understands the human-animal bond well. As a retired veterinarian, teacher, and researcher of the College of Veterinary Medicine at the University of Illinois, he concentrated on companion animal and human bonds for thirty-five years. He continues to devote time to fostering that understanding in veterinary students today.

I would like to write an interview/profile of Erwin Small, DVM, for *Modern Maturity*. "Erv" Small, a short bull of a man, a stub of a cigar often jutting from his mouth, cares deeply for his students as well as animals. Very few, possibly no veterinary student, graduates from U. of I. without attracting Dr. Small's personal interest. His dedication to developing veterinarians who care for both the animals they treat and the pet owners is evident. Small offered grief-counseling courses and organized a program for students to work with pets and strays in inner-city Chicago—long before the term "human-animal bond" was popular. Last year Erv Small received the Bustad Companion Animal Veterinarian Award for pioneering work in the human-animal-bond realm. And his work continues.

As daughter of one of Erv Small's veterinary students, I have grown up hearing his name and met him at veterinary reunions and conferences. I have access to both interview and photograph Dr. Small. As a writer I have covered a variety of subjects since 1985 including human-interest features, scuba diving, and business and technical topics. I recently completed the booklet, *Construct*, for Gemini Consulting.

I can deliver the completed manuscript within two months after assignment in any length you desire. I look forward to hearing from you.

Sincerely,

Lou A. Wood

COMMENTS

The writer's description of this man helped me visualize him as a real person rather than just a name and title. The writer had a connection to him, and his credits seemed good. I passed this query on to our People editor for a possible profile. She passed on the idea. To date the idea hasn't sold. But, "It opened the door for me at *Cats Magazine*," Wood explains. Although that publication also passed on the profile, an editor urged him to send in other ideas. He pitched a piece on how to extend your cat's longevity—and got a 2,000-word assignment. "That proves a query can win an invitation to submit more."

BRIMFIELD, MA

For someone who is excited by a good lion's paw chair, a one-hundred-year-old quilt, even a 1953 Mickey Mantle baseball card, Brimfield is the equivalent of Mecca. Three times a year, the fields around and through this small central Massachusetts town get taken over by more than three thousand antique dealers and attract about fifty thousand people. It is the nation's biggest flea market and, according to the dealers who come from as far away as Wyoming and China, it is the most important.

This "Weekends" column would focus on a trip to Brimfield, home to great antiques and interesting scenes such as a guy wearing a sign around his neck that reads, "I buy pre-1875 sewing machines" or dealers casing the stalls in teams and keeping in contact with walkie-talkies. Since Brimfield can become overwhelming, we can also take a side trip to some of the area's other attractions. Possible candidates include Old Sturbridge Village, a living history museum of New England in the 1830s, the Russian icons at St. Anne's Shrine, one of the world's great medieval armor collections at Higgins Armory in Worcester, a hike through Brimfield State Forest.

Sincerely,

Susan Goodman

COMMENTS

This query was sent to—and the article published by—*National Geographic Traveler*. It's not only a good query that has interesting detail and has been tailored to a specific publication, but it's also a good example of how to approach a familiar editor with whom you're comfortable. This writer knew the editor well, hence the abbreviated form (it was also accompanied by a short cover letter).

Dear Mr. Wood:

While the nation is mushrooming with theme parks dedicated to the glitzy age of fun and fantasy, there's a spot in South Carolina dedicated to serenity, beauty, and art. Brookgreen Gardens, located in Murrells Inlet, encompasses nine thousand acres of woodland and waterways between the Waccamaw River and Atlantic Ocean. It is the butterfly-shaped sculpture garden filled with lush indigenous plants, trees, and more than five hundred works of sculpture that I propose to write about for *Modern Maturity*.

I can submit the piece in several ways. As a travel story by exploring the artistic wonders of the gardens as well as the low-country lifestyle of Murrells Inlet, known for its seafood (don't let names like "Drunken Jacks" scare you—it's the home of a deliciously wicked she-crab soup) and deep-sea fishing charters.

The piece could be a garden feature for a spring or summer issue. It would tell about the arranging and care of the plants and flowers (translating garden hints for managing a ten-acre garden into usable info for the home garden) and the placement and care of the sculpture pieces. This piece would be accompanied by a sidebar about what is in bloom in what season at Brookgreen.

I can also write it as a general-interest story on Brookgreen history, relating anecdotes about the artists and their sculptures.

Also, it can be written for your regional section as a personality profile. Many Brookgreen volunteers are older Americans like retired school principal Dee Reisert who said, "I came to the gardens to read a book and have been here ever since." Color transparencies and information sidebars will accompany the article, no matter what the slant.

The Brookgreen Sculpture Garden was the dream of Archer Huntington and his wife Anna Hyatt Huntington, a famous sculptor. They purchased the land, once the site of four rice plantations, in 1931. By 1932 the sculpture garden was opened to the public. Since then, Brookgreen made the National Register of Historic Places and became a National Historic Landmark in October 1992.

Now after all of the above I'll introduce myself. I'm a freelancer with twenty-five years of newspaper experience as a reporter and editor. The last five career years were as editor of the *Golden Times*, a senior-citizen newspaper in Upstate New York. I have published in *Balloon Life Magazine* and in regional magazines, *Genesee Country* and *Finger Lakes*. My credentials for doing a piece on Brookgreen are my five visits to the gardens during my nine-year acquaintance with Murrells Inlet.

Thank you for your time in listening to my ideas. I can be reached at [number] if you have any questions.

Sincerely,

Joan Merkel Smith

COMMENTS

This has just about everything an editor would want to see: an idea targeted clearly to our magazine's readers, a colorful and detailed—and concise—presentation, a myriad of options, and qualifications that match the concept. I passed it immediately to our Regional editor. Although she rejected the idea, she agreed it was well written. "I passed on it because of the subject rather than the writer or the way she would handle the piece," the Regional editor said. "I'm sure she'd do a good job, but the idea of a sculpture garden didn't excite me. Good for *Southern Living* or *Home & Gardens* maybe, but not us."

Dear Mr. Wood:

Stockyards City. There is no other place like it. Located in the suburbs of Oklahoma City, this famed historical district was founded eighty-four years ago, primarily to service the meat-packing industry in the adjacent stockyards.

Here, the visitor can attend a livestock auction; eat a twenty-ounce steak; order a hand-crafted saddle; buy a conestoga wagon; or stock up on pearl-buttoned shirts and cowboy boots.

"For those looking for the old-time businesses, you'll see more of them here than on any western movie lot," says Chris Wilson, Program Director of Stockyards City Main Street. "The thing is all of them are still in business. This is the real thing."

Also in December, the Stockyards City visitor can participate in Cowboy Christmas with western Christmas decorations; see a real cowboy Santa Claus; attend an old-fashioned long-horn cattle drive; enjoy genuine chuckwagon stew; observe western demonstrations and enter-tainment; and attend the nearby International Professional Rodeo Association Finals.

Or come in June during the annual Stockyards Stampede and browse through western arts and crafts booths; watch leather and silver artisans at work; sample a chili cookoff; dance to western music; and see a bull-riding or bull-fighting exhibition.

No matter when you visit, you'll soon find Stockyards City is the place to be for those who have anything to do with horses or cattle. Home of the working cowboy, it is where the real West still begins.

How did Stockyards City come into being? What makes it so special? How do the stock-yards operate? Why are they the largest cattle auction in the world? What else is here?

Mr. Wood, I would be pleased to answer all of these questions in my proposed travel article, "Stockyards City: Where the Real West Still Begins." Would you be interested in seeing about 2,000 words? On spec, of course. I can furnish pictures.

I have been freelance writing for thirty-five years. My articles have appeared in many publications nationwide, including the regional section of *Modern Maturity* in the April-May 1994 issue. An Oklahoma City tour guide (Territorial Tours), I know the area well.

Sincerely,

Bonnie Speer

COMMENTS

The writer broke one of my rules—she offered the piece on spec—but she got away with it because I'd never heard of this city, and she gave me a lot of details. I passed it on to our Regional editor. Speer writes: "I always begin with the way I plan to open my article. This way the editor can see whether I can write. I also establish why this subject should interest the reader. I present my outline in a list of questions to be answered in the article, then make my pitch to the editor and establish the availability of pictures. I close with my credentials for writing the article."

Dear Mr. Wood:

Al Gionfriddo. Leon Spinks. Mark Fidrych. Keith Smart. Doug Flutie. Don Larsen.

A national star. An instant hero. And then . . . disappointments, mediocrity, failure. These athletes flashed brightly but oh-so-briefly across the American sports horizon, shining for a single moment, a single game, or maybe even a season. But then reality beckoned. They were good enough to rise above the pack, but they weren't Joe Dimaggio or Joe Frazier, so their moment of glory was just that—a moment.

While their names are frozen indelibly—and written into the history books—in association with their singular accomplishments, these competitors were all young men when they reached the summit and each faced an entire life of dealing with both their supreme successes and their subsequent struggles.

I'd like to do a series of features for your magazine on these men (and women from sports like tennis and golf). This would be more than a simple "Historical Moments" or "Where Are they Now." It would probe deeper, searching for answers on various topics: Do they view themselves as successes or failures—and do they base this judgment on their athletic careers or on their entire lives? Do they relive their past with pleasure or avoid it with bitterness? How do the people around them—friends, colleagues, and strangers—treat them? Was their moment so brief because they were lucky or unlucky, unprepared or unequipped to achieve more? Are there lessons to be learned by other pro athletes and, as important, high school and college athletes, who frequently feel unfulfilled after their playing days end?

As America's relationships with its public figures continues to evolve, I think your readers would find these stories on heroes from the recent and not-so-recent past compelling and provocative. The stories could be written in a variety of styles—some as oral history, some as straightforward profiles and some (on deceased players) as historical essays. Eventually, it could be expanded to include athletes whose one moment was negative—Wrong Way Riegels or Ralph Branca—and to athletes whose stellar careers were overshadowed by a single event, like Bobby Thompson or Bill Buckner.

I am a freelance writer (and former *Variety* reporter) and have written for such publications as *GQ*, *New York*, *New Jersey Monthly*, *Sport*, *Inside Sports*, and *Baseball Digest*. I will call you next week to discuss this idea. Thanks for your time and consideration. I look forward to speaking with you soon.

Sincerely,

Stuart Miller

COMMENTS

This is what I mean by narrowing your idea down to a tiny piece of the whole and making it better. He takes a clichéd concept and breaks it down until he finds a niche that is unique. The editor he sent it to liked it and passed it to me. I liked it and even went farther with it, expanding the concept to include everyday people (not just athletes) to appeal to a broader audience. Unfortunately, it was vetoed by the top brass. I wrote the writer back, told him how much I had liked it, and asked him to send me more ideas. The next time an envelope comes in with his name on it, I'll remember him and open it with anticipation. Isn't that what it's all about? (P.S. The author's original idea was eventually sold and appeared in the August 1995 issue of *Inside Sports*.)

BRINGING THE STONES ALIVE

Skyscrapers sprout up in Manhattan like mushrooms after a rain. So, it is hardly unusual that atop Harlem's Morningside Heights, one more tower is pushing upward. Yet, in an era when most high-rise buildings are tents of glass and metal stretched over steel frames, this tower stands apart. At Amsterdam and 112th Street, a team of stoneworkers are building a Gothic Cathedral.

Wielding boasters, toting pinchers, hoisting limestone block upon limestone block, this crew dips into the thirteenth century for building methods to finish what is already the largest cathedral in the world. Two football fields long, the Episcopalian Cathedral of St. John the Divine is twice the size of Notre Dame of Paris. Its temporary dome is so large that the Statue of Liberty could take up residence and welcome her "huddled masses" from within.

The medieval building techniques are accompanied by an equally archaic timetable. In the six weeks it takes a stonecutter to chisel one block of Indiana limestone into a quatrefoil, construction workers downtown can erect six floors of an office tower.

Any article about St. John's is a story with many parts. First would be a brief look at its history—Cathedral begun in 1892, in use seven years later, construction halted due to World War II and not resumed after because gilding such a grand lily seemed tasteless amidst Harlem's poverty. Then in the late '70s during the city's worst financial crisis, the Diocese decided to resume building as a testimony of faith to New York.

The second part of St. John's story is the use of thirteenth-century technology to construct a thirteenth-century building in twentieth-century America. Before St. John's, the last significant stone building to go up in New York was Rockefeller Center in the early 1930s. The last generation of American stonemasons had literally died off. With only five sheets of drawings from the original architect to offer as a guide, church officials imported a Master Builder from England as well as a Master Mason who was himself the first apprentice at Wells Cathedral in twenty years. The article will describe how you build a medieval cathedral where each stone is designed to fit an individual space and cut so accurately that the entire building—arches and all—can be constructed without mortar.

The third part of the story is perhaps St. John's greatest testimony of faith—looking to the streets of Harlem for their building crew. "There's nothing more solid than a piece of stone and that's what a lot of young people down here don't have—a solid base to work from," says Alan Bird, the project's Master Mason. "But when they come to understand how much of themselves they must put into that piece of stone to get something out of it, they end up feeling proud."

Carol Hazel, former welfare mother of four, echoes Bird's sentiments. "I feel free now. I'm a stonecutter . . . I'm not Carol going someplace to get money I didn't have the chance to earn. 'That's my stone,' I'll be able to say to my grandchildren. I'll do this job right."

The photographs for this story could be exotic and varied. Certainly seeing carvers wield this ancient technology would be something new for your readers. Also the Cathedral's carvings, done in a style they've dubbed "Thirteenth-century American gothic," are quite a sight. On the West Portico, for example, Armageddon is portrayed as exploding New York landmarks amidst a mushroom cloud. Jacob's ladder, in his climb to Heaven, is literally the ladder of life, DNA's double helix.

Sincerely,

Susan Goodman

COMMENTS

This is a good example of how to zoom in on an idea. A writer contemplating this topic could have pitched it any number of ways: cathedrals, New York cathedrals, Harlem cathedrals, St. John's cathedral. But Goodman goes even farther, narrowing her focus to the ancient construction style of St. John's cathedral and the resulting community involvement that the project inspired. Like the stones she writes about, there will always be a place for an idea this well-honed and crafted—it even includes quotes that bring the story alive. Although *Action Track* magazine assigned this piece, the publication, alas, changed format shortly afterward and the piece never appeared.

Hello Mr. Wood:

My name is Bruce Selcraig. I've been a journalist twenty years—formerly with both Dallas newspapers and *Sports Illustrated*—and have, since 1989, been freelancing for *Harper's*, the *New York Times Magazine*, *Sierra*, *Los Angeles Times Magazine*, *Columbia Journalism Review*, and others.

I've got a story idea I'd like to run past you.

First, in the past two years I have written occasionally about the environmental problems of golf courses. Some use too much water or pesticides, others displace too much soil during construction. Most are simply not as inviting to nature as we imagine (and developers say) they are. But in isolated cases some golfers have actually been quite seriously injured by chemical exposure on golf courses. They range across the age spectrum, but seniors are usually affected the most.

I think it's time for a serious assessment of what risks the average senior golfer faces on his or her favorite golf course. I should say first that while I consider myself an environmentalist, I am a heavily addicted golfer. I do not believe most golfers have anything to fear from occasional exposure to golf-course chemicals—this is borne out by the relatively few cases of poisonings—and the benefits of the exercise (if they walk) are substantial. However, every golfer, regardless of age, should know about what chemicals a golf course uses, what things never to do (put a tee in one's mouth, for example), and how their favorite golf course can be made safer for the public by decreasing its dependence upon chemicals.

In my years of playing golf I've found golfers to be generally quite unconcerned about the environmental impact of their game. They will drive their golf carts through pristine prairies and fragile wetlands to search for a lost ball. More dangerous, however, is the country-club golfer's insistence that his course resemble the weedless, wall-to-wall green carpets he sees on televised golf tournaments. Not a brown patch anywhere, he says, and look at those greens! They're like pool tables. I'm paying a fortune for my club membership and dues. I want my course to look like that. The only problem, of course, is that this "look" cannot be achieved without abundant use of chemicals.

Even the golf-course superintendents of America recognize this problem, and some have publicly called for golfers to develop a tolerance for occasional weeds, browner grass, and longer, slower greens. (Shorter greens make your putts roll better, but the grass is so short, less than one-tenth of an inch, it constantly battles for survival and so must be soaked with fertilizers and fungus-killing chemicals.) My story would touch on the common problems that many courses present, what progressive golf leaders are doing to make the game healthier, what's really behind the new "environmentally sound" golf courses, and finally, I would urge your readership to become part of a national trend to return golf to its healthier Scottish heritage and learn that demands for flawless green masterpieces increase all our chances—especially golf-course workers—of being unnecessarily exposed to toxics. Not alarmist, just informative, and backed by solid research from agronomists, toxicologists, and physicians. Thanks.

Bruce Selcraig

COMMENTS

This writer begins not with a sparkling lead or a description of his idea, but with his credits. Unusual—and risky—but fortunately the credits he mentions (as well as the clips he attached) are impressive enough to make most editors sit back and read on. His idea is offbeat, intriguing, and appealing to our readers for a number of reasons (health, environment, golf). I had previously been the magazine's Health editor for eight years and had never heard of this danger. This is an excellent example of a fresh idea narrowly focused. I passed it on to our current Health editor with the note "Interesting health idea and good writer prospect."

Although his idea didn't interest her, she thought he might be ideal for a health/environment story she was planning on the medicinal aspects of plants (which goes to show that editors covet good writers more than good ideas). She called him and discovered he knew the subject well. He got the assignment.

Selcraig writes: "Like most writers, I think the query is about one-third of the battle. Aspiring writers should treat the preparation of a query as a science. I have included another query you may want to look at. It is longer than the one you are using, but it is more typical of the ones I, and many other investigative or explanatory journalists, write. The idea that every query should be one page is strictly J-School 101 stuff. I'm not advocating three-page tomes, but complicated stories need to be fully explained."

That should come as a relief to those of you who tend to write long! To see how he did it, see the letter on the next two pages.

Jonathan King
Sierra
730 Polk Street
San Francisco, CA 94109

Hello Jon:

When Bill Grieder of *Rolling Stone* wrote about the free-trade agreement earlier this year, the first two words of his column were: Domingo Gonzales. When ABC's *Prime Time Live* did its investigation of the tragic anencephalic births in Brownsville-Matamoros, the first person they called was Domingo Gonzales. Ditto for the *Chicago Tribune*, National Public Radio, the *New York Times*, CNN, WMAQ-TV, and scores of other reporters, including yours truly.

Gonzales is a calm thoughtful fellow, a former Quaker activist, who upon returning to his native Brownsville from Philadelphia some five years ago, decided he would devote his energies to representing the poor colonias along the border. (See my enclosed story, "Up Against the Wall.") He became the point man for the Coalition for Justice in the Maquiladoras, a group of church and labor organizations working to make the U.S.-owned industries in Mexico behave more responsibly.

So far that's pretty tame stuff—newspaper feature material. But what would make this a fascinating profile (not just a fawning tribute) would be to get inside the head of an activist, to discuss the strategies of confronting corporations, manipulating the media, helping illiterate people to take more control over their lives. He has been a one-man anti-NAFTA machine who puts fear into corporations. How does he target companies? Are some unfairly targeted merely because they are prominent U.S. corporations, as opposed to smaller ones that pollute more? He'll talk about reporters and the questions they ask, their mindset, the requirements of TV and print photographers. ("Would you bring the crying baby closer to the leaking chemical tank, please?")

Specifically, Gonzales has orchestrated marches, boycotts, and media campaigns against U.S.-owned manufacturing plants in Matamoros that are behaving irresponsibly toward workers or the nearby communities. He brought a public-interest toxics lab to Matamoros and conducted tests on the ditches flowing out of several maquiladoras, such as Ford, DuPont and Chicago-based Stepan Chemical. With Stepan, which makes cleansing agents for detergents, the lab found a blood-red, xylene-tainted trench leading out of its property. The video was startling, as were the lab results.

Gonzales alerted the Chicago media as well as a Chicago congresswoman. They met with Stepan officials in Chicago. Stepan bosses flew down to Matamoros. Angry Matamoros mothers confronted them. Classic environmental protest theatre. Stepan made many changes and is now heavily monitored. Stepan hated Gonzales's tactics, thought they were sensational and, at times, defamatory. But Gonzales got what the community needed when everyone else, including the Mexican government, had failed. One chemical company closed, in part due to the constant bad publicity he generated.

That's the story—inside one man's struggle to change corporate policy along the border, and how it is often done with media theatre rather than complicated regulatory and legislative efforts. This would not be a retelling of all the health problems along the border, though that would have to be part of the underlying story.

There are great anecdotes and scenes. Gonzales gets arrested for bringing toxic waste to an EPA press conference. Gonzales leads angry mothers to confront Mexican officials. Gonzales walks his family's old farm, which has become surrounded by agribusiness and commercial sprawl, while threatened by the pollution and mismanagement of the Rio Grande. Fantastic photos, like Domingo walking the railroad tracks behind chemical plants, laughing with children swimming in a polluted ditch. (I've taken some of these myself.) He may also have a very good reason to fear for his life. His campaigns can seriously threaten profits, and Matamoros is a notoriously dangerous town for activists and labor leaders.

The whole key to pulling this story off would be to make it less the story of a crusader, and more the story of how one properly crusades. I think his introspection and candor about what he does will make the story.

I'll call you soon.

Bruce Selcraig

COMMENTS

Reading a query as well-crafted as this one is almost like reading the article itself. What a story, what a person, what visual possibilities (editors are always envisioning what a piece will look like as well as read like). It's drenched with color and images and people and horrors and emotions. The writer immersed himself so completely in this saga that he left no doubt he knew this story better than anyone else and could pull it off. "Border Patrol" appeared in the May/June 1994 issue of *Sierra*.

Dear Mr. Wood:

A thirty-year veteran of the San Luis Obispo, California, fire department has found a highly satisfying—and unusual—second career as museum restorator at the Hall of Flame in Phoenix, Arizona, the nation's largest museum of firefighting. Since 1980, Don Hale (now around 70) has restored several fire vehicles, most recently a 1951 Mack fire engine from the town of Eagle Valley, New York.

Mr. Hale would make a great profile for your publication, weaving accounts of his days battling real flames with the meticulous work of restoration. Also, photos of Mr. Hale with restored fire vehicles would be very dramatic.

I am a full-tiime freelance writer and photographer with multiple bylines in the *Chicago Tribune*, the *South Bend Tribune*, and the *Fort Wayne News-Sentinel*. My magazine features include *Notre Dame Magazine*, *Home & Away*, *MotorHome*, and *Career World*.

I look forward to your response.

Sincerely,

Bob Kronemyer

COMMENTS

This letter is concise, yet full of details and color. It's customized to our magazine in general and to our regional section in particular. It provides options: It could work as either a profile of the museum or the restorator. And the writer's bio is impressive. I passed this query on to both our Regional and People editors.

Dear Mr. Wood:

Enclosed is a query for an article on pain that I'd like to write for *Modern Maturity*. As I'm sure you know, the fast-growing elderly population of the United States is forcing recognition that more and more people are living with chronic illnesses, many of which involve pain. Few people know, however, that most pain can be successfully managed with treatments that are already available. As Dr. Betty Ferrell of the City of Hope Medical Center told me, "The relief of pain is awaiting no scientific breakthroughs. We have everything we need today to relieve pain."

The article I propose would educate people and help them demand more effective pain management from their medical professionals.

I have been a professional science writer for print and television for the past fifteen years. Last year my book, *Sexual Strategies: How Females Choose Their Mates*, was published by Tarcher/ Putnam. The paperback will be out in January. Currently I am free-lancing for *Self* magazine and *Cosmopolitan*.

I look forward to hearing from you.

Sincerely,

Mary Batten

QUERY FOR ARTICLE ON PAIN: THE INVISIBLE PROBLEM

Almost everyone has had or will have some experience with pain—the suffering of a child, the long-term illness of a parent, or the helpless feeling of one's own pain. Pain is the most prevalent symptom of many illnesses, but until recently it was the last symptom to be treated.

Once called the "invisible problem," pain is finally beginning to be taken seriously as a major medical problem affecting great numbers of people. Among other things, the fast-growing elderly population in the United States is forcing recognition that more and more people are living with chronic illnesses that will not disappear and go away, illnesses that will not be cured. Many of these illnesses, most notably cancer, involve pain.

Many people fear pain more than disease, but few know that pain can be effectively managed. For example, 95 percent of cancer pain can be effectively relieved. The best news, however, is that pain management does not require the discovery of a "magic bullet" or a miracle drug.

Why then aren't more patients demanding effective pain relief? Lack of education—and fear. Fear of drug addiction is the major barrier among consumers. People feel they have to choose either to have pain or to be knocked out by pain-killers. In fact, this is not the case; there *are* other options. Fewer than one percent of patients with chronic severe pain become addicted. But these facts are not widely disseminated. Even terminal patients fear addiction and say they don't want to die a junkie. This fear, of course, has been conditioned by society's "Just Say No to Drugs" admonition. There's a bitter irony: While the illegal drug trade flourishes, cancer patients suffer needlessly by refusing prescribed medication or taking less medication than the amount needed to give them comfort and enhance their quality of life.

Doctors and nurses, too, need better education in pain management. According to studies, the average medical student will graduate in 1993 from the best medical schools in America having received only one hour of content devoted to pain. The average nursing student will graduate from the best nursing schools in America having received only 3.9 hours of content devoted to pain.

Fortunately both professional and consumer awareness of the need for pain management is being raised. Nationally and internationally, in the past four years, pain has been identified as a priority for research by the American Cancer Society, the National Institutes of Health, the Agency for Health Care Policy and Research, and the World Health Organization. New cancer-pain guidelines were just released by the federal Agency for Health Care Policy and Research. This is only a beginning, however. Much remains to be done, and some professionals see consumer education as the key, pointing out that when consumers demand better treatment, the medical community responds.

Various National Center Institute Designated Clinical Cancer Research Centers are pursuing aggressive institution-wide approaches to pain management. These multifaceted programs involve free educational seminars for patients and their families and in-house education for staff nurses and doctors. The focus is on the patient as a whole human being and not just a disease carrier. "Pain is not just a physical event. Pain is more than a tumor. There are the physical, emotional, and spiritual aspects," says Paul Coluzzi, M.D., Chief of the City of Hope's recently established Supportive Care Service.

Knowledge is power. When patients and their families receive pain education, they can participate more fully as partners in their care. The result is significant improvement in their quality of life.

Through interviews with doctors, nurses, and patients at various pain centers throughout the United States, and a review of the literature, this article will explore the myths about pain and new approaches to relieving it.

COMMENTS

Queries, by their very nature, don't need cover letters. But some writers, like this one, prefer to separate their introductory remarks and personal biographical information from their article ideas. This allows their article idea to shine alone. I don't recommend this procedure with magazine queries because it's unnecessary, takes more work, adds more paperwork, and may upset an impatient editor. But I included it to let you see its advantages, too. This submission was forwarded to our Health editor, who liked its detail, quotes, research, and writing style. "Take Charge of Your Pain" appeared in our January-February 1995 issue.

Dear Mr. Wood:

I'd like to introduce myself and suggest a project to you that I think would have great appeal for readers of *Modern Maturity* (of which, being an AARP member, I am a diligent reader).

I am a retired journalist (resume attached) who now supplements his pension and Social Security income by freelance writing, book reviewing, teaching, lecturing, and other pursuits. Over my working years I worked for the *New Bedford Standard-Times*, the *Akron Beacon Journal*, and, from 1964 to 1992, the *Cleveland Plain Dealer*, where I won several national awards while functioning as music critic.

For many years I have been a frequenter of the Chautauqua Institution in extreme western New York State, both as guest and as participant in programs there. It seems to me that this unusual place, which generally caters to an older clientele, would be a natural for a feature story in *Modern Maturity*. You see people of all ages there, but there is a heavy preponderance of older folks.

Chautauqua is a privately operated self-contained little community on the shore of a beautiful lake. It offers all the usual attractions of a lakeside resort—boating, swimming, fishing, etc.—but in addition a staggering list of lectures, seminars, discussion groups, literary activities, and religious offerings during its annual nine-week season. There is a full professional symphony orchestra there, an opera company, a ballet company, and a theater troupe. Chautauqua was founded some 125 years ago as a training ground for Sunday school teachers and there is still a heavy religious emphasis there, but there are no restrictions on who may attend or on what they may do when they get there. You can go sailing if you want, or attend a lecture on conditons inside the former Soviet Union—or just sit on your porch and read a good book (it doesn't even have to be a GOOD book—no one will check up on you!). Horace Deets, executive director of AARP, has spoken there at least once.

My wife and I just spent two days there, and in that short time we (1) heard a fascinating lecture by a Holocaust survivor; (2) heard a talk by a cardiologist on the life and work of Lewis Thomas; (3) heard an excellent symphony concert; (4) attended a very good production of Shakespeare's "The Tempest"; (5) looked in on the institution's new chamber music hall; (6) greeted friends, old and new, on the walkways, in the shops, and at the dining table.

There is an old-fashioned air about Chautauqua, a quaintness that those in charge are trying very hard to preserve. When you walk through that gate, it's as though eighty or ninety years have somehow dropped off the calendar. The institution draws people from all over the country during its summer season, with heavy representation from the nearby cities of Cleveland, Buffalo, and Pittsburgh. There are also several hundred people who own property there and live there all summer long.

If you agree with me that this unusual place would make a good feature subject for *Modern Maturity*, I hope you'll contact me so we can discuss length, editorial slant, art possibilities (payment, too!). I should add that I have no official connection with Chautauqua, though I have on two occasions over the years been a participant in programs there. The 1994 summer season is already in full swing, so I assume you might schedule a story for the spring of 1995 to coincide with the 1995 opening, which will be at the end of June, if past practice is followed.

I look forward to hearing from you.

Cordially,

Robert Finn

COMMENTS

You can tell this writer really knows and likes this place. I did, too. You get a clear picture of the town, its people, its activities. In addition, the writer took into consideration the magazine's typical long lead time by sending us his query well in advance and by suggesting when it might best fit in. It seemed like a natural for us, the writer's credentials were solid, and I passed it on to our Regional editor.

Dear Mr. Gordon:

What happens when high technology lets you down? SimuFlite Training International recently faced this question head-on. Located at D/FW Airport, SimuFlite burst on the scene in 1982, the largest aviation start-up in history, a company that specializes in training for corporate, commercial, and military pilots. Nuclei of its training programs: the most advanced aircraft simulators available and computer-based (CBT) groundschool—both of which set SimuFlite apart from a company that dominated the pilot-training market for years.

Yet SimuFlite barely opened its doors before resistance to CBT appeared. After several years of efforts to wean pilots from traditional stand-up instruction to its "FasTrak Personal Education System," SimuFlite gave up the fight. Says George Ferito, Vice President of Business Aviation, "It almost cost us our existence."

Why did high-tech professional pilots resist CBT? How did SimuFlite try to offset their objections? What finally spurred the company to execute a courageous (and costly) about-face, reshaping course content for 100 percent instructor-led presentation? The answers to these questions spotlight the curious tension between humans and high technology, and form the basis for a story I'd like to write for *Training*: "Turnaround in Mid-Flight: How SimuFlite Averted a Corporate Crash."

My sources include V.P. Ferito and training specialists involved in initial and restructured course development. My qualifications include a long-time association with the company. As a freelancer, I wrote the SimuFlite newsletter for several years (I'm enclosing a back issue) and articles for the aviation press.

I can have the SimuFlite story ready within six weeks of your go-ahead. Thanks for your time.

Sincerely,

Connie Bovier

COMMENTS

This letter was presented by Ms. Bovier as part of her workshop at the Twelveth Annual "Craft of Writing" conference held in Dallas in 1994. Its first paragraph hooks the reader, the second and third 'graphs provide the meat of the article, the fourth 'graph gives the sources and writer credentials, and the last 'graph explains the timing. "How a High-Tech Training System Crashed and Burned" appeared in the August 1993 issue of *Training* magazine.

Dear Mr. Wood:

Right now the future looks pretty slim for our nation's seniors. And we owe it all to Generation X. They are rapidly taking over with their nose rings, combat boots, lazy attitudes, and shallow aspirations.

Wake up America! We're not all bad. I am an official member of Generation X (born in the seventies) and I am sure I am not the only X'er who has a college degree, a full-time job, a clean-cut style, and a great deal of respect for those who came before me. Just ask my Grandma.

I have written a 1,500-word article about my grandmother (a *Modern Maturity* reader) and the valuable lessons of life she has passed on to me. Even though, according to many people in today's society, I am supposed to think my grandmother and her values are ridiculous and outdated, I treasure the unique relationship I have with her. She has taught me about people, patience, tolerance, integrity, and love.

The readers of your magazine will enjoy reading a refreshing story about the love between a grandmother and her young adult granddaughter. Perhaps the timely element will make them feel more confident about the future of their own grandchildren and great-grandchildren.

My background includes a degree in journalism from the University of Maryland at College Park. In May of 1993 I graduated magna cum laude. I am currently an assistant account executive for a public-relations firm in Baltimore, Maryland. On a daily basis, I work with the American Geriatrics Society, where I focus my efforts on improving the health and well-being of our growing senior population.

I look forward to hearing from you soon. Thank you.

Sincerely,

Rosemary Ostmann

COMMENTS

From a "say what?" lead that grabbed my attention, to a brief but informative description of the piece being offered, to a short bio pertinent to the topic and my magazine, no editor could hope for more. I immediately asked Ms. Ostmann to send me the article in question.

Dear Mr. Wood:

As a reporter with the *Chicago Sun-Times*, I have covered everything from corruption trials to computer shopping. I have also managed to write some free-lance magazine pieces on the side.

I propose an article for *Modern Maturity* on some facet of my seventy-seven-year-old mother's visit to a fitness resort, or what it's like for "Ma at the Spa."

Next week my mother and I will be visiting Canyon Ranch in Tucson, Arizona, where she will participate in their wellness program for seniors. This will be a first-time experience for a woman who does not exercise and is extremely overweight. I have been at Canyon Ranch several times in the past, but am very interested in what they will offer my mother.

Possible story ideas include: (a) some account of what it was like to see my mother take part in such a program in a role reversal of all those times in the past when she dragged her now forty-five-year-old daughter to ballet classes and cultural events; (b) A diary as recounted by her to me of a stay at a fitness ranch which caters to people of all ages and what she found there; (c) A story on her visit and its aftermath; or (d) A story on her experience coupled with that of other retirees or seniors who are also in attendance. I will take pictures of her visit, of course.

I think one of these ideas (or yet another) would appeal to your readers, and I am excited about writing for *Modern Maturity*. I have enclosed some clips to give you some idea of my writing.

Thank you for your time and consideration. I hope to hear from you soon.

Sincerely,
Adrienne Drell

COMMENTS

Everyone liked this idea, particularly the *a* angle. The writer presents it nicely—a short personal introduction to whet our appetite; a synopsis of the article; the logistics of what, when, and where; some alternative angles; and a standard, polite close. "Duel in the Sun" appeared in our April-May 1993 issue.

Dear Mr. Wood:

She has never been to school. Never. But, of course, this was not expected. She made her debut at Buckingham Palace.

Safely outside the palace gates, she read *Out of Bounds; The Education of Giles and Esmond Romilly*. This eyewitness account excoriated the famed English public school. Shamelessly, she became smitten with one of the authors—whom she had yet to meet—and decided he was going to be her man. Her parents, she knew, would not be amused. So, under strict family supervision, the bride and groom to-be met for the first time in a country house drawing room. They exchanged blood oaths, then hatched a plan. They would elope and report on the Spanish Civil War.

The groom was Winston Churchill's nephew.

Only weeks before she had read accounts of his defense of Spain in the International Brigade; but now, it was their wedding that hastened an international crisis.

The bride, herself, was Churchill's cousin.

Her parents, ancient peers-of-the-realm, flexed weighty muscles, and Britain, as a consequence, threatened to withhold aid to Basque women and children being evacuated from the war zone. Said the bride, later, of the blackmail, "This shabby piece of bargaining brought home to me the strength and ruthlessness of the forces ranged against us." In 1941 the groom—then a pilot in the Royal Canadian Air Force—disappeared over the North Sea.

Fast forward. 1951. With a cadre of four comrades, she donned hats, stockings, white gloves and crossed the Mississippi border into the shadows of the Ku Klux Klan. Willie Magee, thirty-six, had been charged with raping a woman. The only evidence was the man was black and the woman was white. Prevailing upon the Southern myth of the sanctity of white women, these members of the American Communist Party traversed the state on a mission of justice. Save for the help of novelist William Faulkner, their support was, literally, "just us."

Fast forward. 1955. Montgomery, Alabama. The night after the bus boycotts she joined Martin Luther King, Jr., in a sweltering church. Meanwhile, outside, the National Guard kept an unruly mob at bay. Those inside the church were advised not to leave before dawn. All night long they sang hymns. Dispatches arrived regularly with news: The church was to be torched, a car had been burned. At daybreak, they filed out. The burned car was hers. The National Guard, guns drawn, escorted her to safety in a jeep.

Fast forward. 1970. The *Atlantic* published her exposé on "The Famous Writer's School." That edition became the magazine's best-selling issue to date. Her devastating dissection prompted "the school" to file bankruptcy proceedings.

Her older sister, Nancy, was the popular novelist—part of the "Bright Young People" (so called by newspapers), whose members numbered, among others, Evelyn Waugh—while yet, another sister, Unity, was a friend of Hitler. The day upon which England declared war, this sister, firmly entrenched in Germany, shot herself in the head with a gun bought expressly for this purpose. Her youngest sister is the present Duchess of Devonshire. For decades, this wildly eccentric family has grabbed world headlines. They were even subjects of an English musical.

But this daughter of the aristocracy is no blue stocking. Bored, she traded her tiara for a shovel. *Time* magazine, consequently, dubbed her "Queen of the muckrakers," the only title she glories in. The daughter of Lord and Lady Redesdale, her most famous work exhumed sharp business practices in the funeral industry in the vivid exposé, *The American Way of Death* (1963). She has come full circle. Now, *The American Way of Birth* (1992) dares the medical establishment. With astringent precision and razor-sharp wit—her trademarks—Jessica Mitford details the history of American childbirth from the nineteenth century to the present. She says: "Commerical interests are essential to consider when trying to understand the spread of a new technique." Mitford, eyes ablaze, points to a standard medical textbook in 1937 which states with certainty that X-rays pose no danger to the fetus. "Advocates of a new technique are liable to suffer from a strange condition called certainty," she said.

Not long ago, Maya Angelou was invited to open a circus. Her task was to ride into the center ring seated astride an elephant. She consented only on one condition—that her friend, Jessica Mitford, accompany her.

Said former *Washington Post* reporter, Carl Bernstein, of *Poison Penmanship: The Gentle Art of Muckraking* (1979): "Ms. Mitford demystifies what should be a simple process and takes us back to the basics. Reporting, she knows, is the best obtainable version of the truth. Then she shows us how to get there with grace, wit, cunning, style, imagination, and—above all—a sense of enjoying the journey."

Recently, I had the pleasure of dining with Jessica Mitford. The National Endowment for the Humanities is sponsoring her lecture series. Mitford's common sense, unfailing wit, and ethical approach continue to excise sacred cows. The public is thus better informed about its choices. Jessica Mitford's other books include *The Trial of Dr. Spock* (1969) and *Kind and Usual Punishment* (1979). I propose an interview. Ms. Mitford, an American citizen, has kindly agreed.

My work has appeared in *The Times of London*, *Essence Magazine*, *The Commerical Appeal*, *Mississippi Magazine*, the *New Orleans Tribune*, and weekly newspapers in America. Thank you for your time. I look forward to your reply.

Yours sincerely,

Joseph Dumas

COMMENTS

Whew! That's a query letter. In fact, it is quite possibly the finest one I have ever read. Although it is exceedingly long and waits until the bottom of the second page to divulge its topic—both suicidal habits—you can't put it down. It reads like a novel. This writer did his homework, this writer painted a picture, this writer was passionate about his subject. And this writer got a four-thousand-dollar assignment. I knew nothing about Mitford until I got this letter; after reading it, I was desperate to know more. If you want an exemplar query letter to study and pattern yours after (with the exception of the two no-nos—other editors may not be so forgiving), you can't do much better than this one.

Dear Mr. Brohaugh:

As you well know, every beginning magazine freelancer has a wish list—from the practical ("I wish I knew what every editor wants") to the impractical ("I wish I could sell everything I write") to the absurd ("I wish my first sale is read by a powerful agent who persuades me to turn it into a novel, which becomes a best-seller that's sold to Hollywood, which Spielberg options and begs me to let him direct").

You've explored these kinds of wishes in *Writer's Digest* for years, but there's one I don't think you've examined yet: that of a magazine editor. As senior editor of *Dynamic Years* (which has ranked high on your top freelance-market list for several years) and a former freelancer myself, I, too, have my share of wishes and dreams—from the practical to the impractical to the, yes, even absurd—which I'd like to share with your readers.

My 1,500-word "Ten Wishes Every Editor Wants" (which could be written as a theme for Christmas or New Year's resolution time) outlines not only what every editor dreams about every time he picks up a new manuscript, but how writers can achieve their dreams, too, if only they knew what editors are looking for. Each example below will include anecdotes, advice, and/or actual examples of wishes that came true or went unfulfilled—and why. My wish list includes the following:

1. *I wish I could buy everything that comes in.* Although every editor says this, few freelancers believe it (I know I never did). Well, I'd like to set the record straight. I'll show how eager we really are to buy their work.

2. *I wish I could show favoritism to friends, staff, or previously published writers.* Contrary to popular opinion, good editors don't. Their only concern is what's good for the magazine. Period. Every time, all the time, and I'll explain why.

3. *I wish I could get back to writers ASAP.* Deadlines, meetings, slow decision-making, and small staffs all work against speedy replies, but do writers believe this? They will after they read what really goes on.

4. *I wish writers knew how easy we really are.* It's amazing how eagerly we gobble articles that are right, that are new, that are queried professionally. If only I knew then (when I was freelancing) what I know now! Now your readers will know.

5. *I wish I could tell from just a query idea if the writer's right for it.* Unfortunately, editors need more convincing: clips, prior articles sold (and where to), work experience or background that proves why you're best qualified to pull it off, etc. Joe Friday would have been a good editor: "Just the facts, ma'am."

6. *I wish writers would do what they say they'll do.* But editors get only so many miracles in one lifetime. Rarely does a writer fulfill every promise made in a query. Don't writers realize they could elevate themselves to god status if they'd just perform this one task? If my examples

don't convince them, nothing will.

7. *I wish I knew the perfect writer for my magazine.* But that's a pipe dream. Nobody knows my readers better than I do, writes with style and passion, researches meticulously, meets deadlines, is willing to rewrite, or throws in occasional bonuses (like extra sidebars or info beyond what was asked for). Or do they?

8. *I wish I knew the perfect subject matter for my magazine.* Editors aren't psychics. We don't have time to drum up ideas all day. We're too busy editing, phoning, going to meetings, etc. Successful writers, however, do that for us. They study our magazine, dream our dreams, and become, in a sense, our real editors. I'll show the magic that results when such a prized writer is found.

9. *I wish I knew a writer who was as passionate about my magazine as I am.* But there ain't no such animal. At least, I haven't found one yet. When I do, he or she will work for me forever. Or take my place. Don't believe me? How do you think I got my job?

10. *I wish I was the perfect editor for every writer.* But I'm not perfect, either. Heaven knows, I've made my share of mistakes, but a good editor learns from them. I'll share a few of my choicest foul-ups.

Is this idea just wishful thinking on my part, or is it perhaps a rare opportunity to let your readers look at their manuscripts from an editor's point of view? My work has appeared in such publications as *Off Duty*, *Basketball Digest* and, of course, *Dynamic Years*. If you'd like my wish list, I could deliver it within two weeks of assignment.

Sincerely,

John Wood

COMMENTS

This was my first query—and sale—to *Writer's Digest* way back in 1985. Since then I've sold numerous pieces to them. The editor I sent it to is now editor of Writer's Digest Books, who subsequently offered me the opportunity to write the book you're reading. So, who knows what one query may lead to!

Questions & Answers

Q: I regularly obey your Ten Commandments, yet most of my queries still get rejected. How come?

A: You've just identified the saddest fact of life about the writing profession. You've also discovered why writing, like acting, is one of the most difficult careers to excel in. Why does it happen? Let's take a hypothetical example. You send *GQ* a query on a profile of Daniel Day-Lewis. You've followed every Commandment. The profile editor reads your query, is intrigued by your research, the effort you put into it, your professionalism, your background, etc. But she just bought a Daniel Day-Lewis piece a month ago. If she's a considerate editor, she'll jot a note onto your letter explaining this fact, say she was impressed with your clips and presentation and ask to see more ideas from you. If she's pressed for time and not so thoughtful, she'll just reject it, you'll get a form letter back, and you'll wonder what the hell you did wrong—especially when you see a Daniel Day-Lewis profile appear soon after in that magazine.

Here are just some of the many reasons why bad things happen to good queries:

Bad timing. The publication has just bought something similar, is planning to do something similar with another writer, or a competing publication just did or is about to do something similar.

Overstocked. The publication can't afford to buy any new material until the majority of its current inventory is depleted. If it made an exception every time a good idea came in (such as yours), its inventory would pile up and everything would soon be outdated.

Overbudget. The publication has bought too much material and cannot assign any new articles until the next fiscal period.

Change in editorial direction. The publication has had a recent change in policy, a new editor/publisher, a redesign, or was or is about to be bought out by a conglomerate. Bottom line: It's changed course, or is contemplating doing so, and will no longer look like the current newsstand version. Therefore, it isn't buying anything until the dust settles and a new course is charted.

The editor is an idiot. This is my personal favorite and, I'm sure, yours. You've done everything right, your idea's fresh, you've got the right stuff, but the editor just shrugs. What can I say, other than you and your query will forever be at the whim of an editor's mood, age, sex, race, nationality, income level, and personal preferences. What's the solution? I don't have one. All I can say is that editors are human, thank goodness there are so many of them, try again, and send it elsewhere.

Q: How helpful are "writer's guidelines" when researching a magazine?

A: Next to zero. A typical "writer's guidelines" sheet is outdated, inaccurate, overgeneralized, and not worth the time or effort to obtain. Here's a typical one: "We're looking for humor, consumer, and travel pieces between 1,000 and 3,000 words geared to women twenty-four through thirty-six." You could guess that from the magazine cover—and a lot more if you research the publication yourself. Most guidelines are worthless because they're rarely updated. That's because it would cost too much to redo and reprint them every time some in-house editorial policy changed. And magazines evolve constantly. They change editors, staffs, departments, design, and editorial direction every few years, not to mention countless minor adjustments every issue, so to rely on their guidelines for accurate marketing information is like choosing what movie to see from last year's newspaper.

Q: You say it's important to focus my query idea, but how much should I shrink it? Can an idea ever be *too* narrow for an article?

A: From my experience, it's always better to err on compressing an idea too much than too little. If I see a query I like that's too focused, I have two options—and both are good: (1) I can use the piece for one of my departments or, (2) I can ask you to flesh it out more for a feature article.

Q: Should my queries include a resume?

A: Resumes don't provide editors with any useful information. I don't need to know your entire work and education background, your awards and accomplishments, your career goals, etc. I only want personal facts that pertain to your article idea. And that information should be in your query letter.

Q: Are simultaneous submissions OK?

A: More and more editors are coming around and accepting them today; they're finally acknowledging that writers have a living to make. Editors cannot realistically expect you to wait for weeks or months until, or if, you get their reject letter back before you send it elsewhere. How are you expected to pay your bills in the meantime?

As a courtesy, though, and to cover yourself in case you get lucky and more than one editor responds favorably, I would mention in your letter that you're submitting your query concurrently. That way everybody knows up front what's going on. Not only that, they also know that if they like your idea, they'd better hurry or one of the other editors will grab it first.

Will saying it's a simultaneous submission kill your chances with editors who are offended by them? Probably, but why would you want to work with such Neanderthals?

Q: Are photocopied queries appropriate?

A: One recent how-to book recommended freelance writers use photocopied queries, even postcard queries, with "yes" and "no" boxes at the bottom. I disagree with this advice. You're a professional writer, not a direct-mail advertiser. Always treat editors the way you would prefer to be treated.

Aha, you say. Gotcha! You editors *don't* treat writers the same way! You send us form-letter rejects—sometimes, yes, even postcards—so why should we waste good paper on you?

A fair question, but I'm afraid it's not the same thing. The difference is, we're not writing you first, nor did we ask you to write us. We're simply replying (and not just to you, but to thousands more like you). I can't think of a situation in which an editor, needing or wanting to contact you initially, would do so with a photocopy or a form letter. Would you want to do business with someone like that?

CHAPTER FOUR

The Article Query: The Ten Query Sins

"Here are a few of the unpleasantest words that ever blotted paper!"
Shakespeare

Now that you know what editors want in a query letter, you're all set, right? Wrong. That's only half the battle. I only told you what an editor covets; now I'm going to tell you what an editor loathes—the ten most common query-letter blunders, any one of which may doom your letter to instant rejection.

To some editors, committing a Query Sin is more serious than disobeying one of the cherished Query Commandments. That's because just one of these blasphemous errors has the capability of sending a flawless, inculpable, Commandment-laden query straight to you-know-where faster than you can say, "This does not meet our present needs." If you ever hope to sell to magazines or newspapers, therefore, you must permanently eradicate each and every one of these ten fatal errors from your composition style.

The Ten Query Sins

No query letter must ever be:
1. **Wordy** (text rambles; length exceeds one-and-a-half pages)
2. **Sketchy** (idea isn't fleshed out enough)
3. **Presumptuous** (tone is too cocky)
4. **Egotistical** (topic is yourself)
5. **Reluctant** (lame reason why you're doing it)
6. **Loose-Lipped** (article is offered on spec)

7. **Stubborn** (prior rejects from same editor haven't given you the hint)
8. **Intrusive** (phone call precedes or supplants query)
9. **Inappropriate** (clips don't match the idea)
10. **Careless** (faults are mentioned or major gaffe is made)

Wordy

A longtime rule for query letters is: Keep it to one page. That's still a good rule. Without it, writers might assume they have carte blanche to write a novella—which, given the chance, many would do. Speaker and journalism professor Peter Jacobi likens writers who ramble to people who rent moving vans: "They pack in everything haphazardly, then get lost along the way." The trick, Jacobi says, is to pack so as not to waste space.

TV and film writers often must pitch their ideas hastily (five minutes, tops) when they meet producers. The good ones have perfected these precious moments to a science by devising a catchy "hook" that's easily grasped ("E.T. lost in Jurassic Park"). Then they jump to the plot, concentrating only on their can't-miss scenes and main characters, and finish with a bang (a Ross Perot-like chart showing projected record-breaking box-office receipts is always nice). Sound familiar? It should. That's the ideal formula for a query letter.

Like our producer counterparts, we editors don't have time for writers who take forever to get to the point, who go off on tangents, or who pad their letters with extraneous information. Limiting your letters to one page (or one-and-a-half pages, maximum) accomplishes three objectives: It forces you to write concisely, it helps you focus your idea, and it encourages, rather than discourages, an editor to continue reading. As the old adage goes, if you can't explain your concept in one page, you're not clear about it yourself. Not a strong selling point.

Sketchy

Some writers provide only bare-bones information when describing their idea—and nothing more. A one-sentence "hook" to grab an editor is fine (in fact, it's ideal), but that's just to tease the editor; it should never be the whole thing. But many writers stop at this point and go no farther. I call these "telegram queries" because the writers must think each word describing their concept costs them money. It costs them money all right, but not the way they think.

There are three reasons why writers clam up about their idea, and all are wrong: (1) they don't want their query to run long, (2) they are afraid an editor might steal the details and rip them off, or, (3) they fear the more information they furnish, the more opportunities an editor will have to reject them. Let's take a look at each fallacy separately.

1. NO TIME FOR DETAILS

One of the cardinal rules of query-writing is *be concise*, but that tenet refers only to the length of the entire letter. Certain parts of your query, such as the article synopsis, can and should be quite detailed (a couple of paragraphs, maximum). Like a car salesman who gives his customers no more than the make and model of his cars, you won't sell many of your products if you gloss over the details.

I once got a query whose idea, in its entirety, was: "Walking tours in San Francisco." The writer then had the nerve to add, "If you're interested, please send me guidelines and I'll get right on it." Right. Get on what? A doctor once queried me who was obviously a fan of the movie *The Graduate*. His proposal consisted of one word: "Dermabrasion."

I understand how difficult it is to compose a query. You're told to cram everything onto one page. But scrimping on the article description, figuring, "If the editor wants to know more about 'rodent taxidermy,' she'll follow up," is going about it backwards.

2. FEAR OF THEFT

A writer once called me to ask why I had rejected his query. I told him he hadn't given any details about his proposal. He said he never did that in his queries. "Why give you my whole story without being paid for it?" he said. I could see his point. Whenever I send out my own queries I, too, instinctively hesitate when I get to the details. How much should I reveal? Is this wise? It's like being on a first date. How much personal information should I lay on this person? Will it turn her off or endear her to me? I was always open, figuring what the hell, she's either going to like me or not. Same with queries. Sure you're vulnerable, but you're going to have to spill the beans sooner or later.

Do editors steal ideas from writers? I'm sure ignorant, lazy, dishonest people lurk in every profession. But don't buy into the myth that most editors are out to rip you off. Most don't have to. Especially editors from the well-known newsstand giants. They have more than enough material, and if they like your idea, they have the bucks to buy it. In fact, they're infamous for racking up enormous "kill-fee" losses every year because they overbuy like mad, then have to ditch a lot of material because it gets outdated. So they're going to steal your gem of an idea to save a few bucks? Many also have deep pockets and realize they're sitting ducks to any writer with a legitimate grievance. A heavy lawsuit, and the resulting loss of prestige, would cost them far more than what they'd save ripping you off.

When "your idea" appears in a publication that earlier rejected it, it's usually not due to theft but to the fact that the idea was popular; the editor probably got twenty clones to your concept during that same period. If theft occurs at all, it most likely happens in small, nondescript publications where you'll find a lot of beginning editors who may not know any better or figure no one will know. Two *Modern Maturity* articles of mine were reprinted in tiny publications without our approval—one even had a staff member's by-line on it.

3. JUST THE FACTS, MA'AM

Some writers flinch at divulging details for fear that the more they reveal, the more excuses they'll give an editor to say no. ("Gee, I loved the first nineteen points in your outline, but that twentieth just turned me off. Sorry.") To avoid this possibility, they show just enough to whet an editor's appetite—and no more.

My response: The prospects you lose by revealing too much will more than offset the ones you win by doing the same. What sane editor would reject a detailed proposal that's exactly what she's looking for just because of a few oddball elements? She'll just ask the writer to change them or take them out. A lot of brainstorming and restructuring between writers and editors goes on before assignments are given the green light. It is a rare assignment whose finished draft mirrors the original concept.

Presumptuous

Never assume an editor will choose cockiness over confidence. Nothing dampens a query more than a phrase like, "Please let me know when you'll send the check so I can look for it." Don't laugh, I see these lines a lot.

That's not to say you shouldn't be optimistic about your queries' chances.

The last thing writers should be is fatalistic and go in halfhearted. When I send one of my queries out, I *know* it's going to sell. How could it possibly fail? At least that's what I tell myself. The difference is, I take care not to strut that self-confidence in my letter. Editors like to think *they* make these decisions.

Therefore, always try to rein in your expectations, even though the anticipation threatens to spill onto your page like an overturned ink bottle. Editors can smell bravado or longing in a letter, and it makes them uneasy. It exposes you as an amateur. Professional writers have queried successfully for so long that the word "anxiety" no longer exists in their lexicon. Their stance: If you don't buy it, fine, somebody else will.

Avoid these presumptuous phrases:

"I've enclosed photos and some options on how to lay out and illustrate the piece." [Never send photos unless you're asked to, but by all means mention that you have some. I would also steer clear of offering any design advice—even editors avoid this minefield—because that is the domain of the publication's art department.]

"It will become clear to you, after reading my proposal, that my idea is a natural for your publication." [Let your concept speak for itself.]

"It has occurred to me that your magazine would be substantially more enjoyable to many of your readers if each issue included a chess column." [These types of suggestions are fine—for a letter to the editor. But they're not appropriate in a query.]

"Let me suggest, even if you have some initial doubts about the idea, that we get together anyway and discuss it." [Very few assignments require a face-to-face meeting between a writer and an editor; even the most involved projects can usually be handled over the phone. That said, no editor is going to meet with you in person to discuss an idea she *doesn't* like.]

"How much do you pay for articles of this type?" [Isn't this putting the cart before the horse? It also alerts the editor that you haven't done even the least bit of research about her publication.]

"Frankly, I've never seen a Christmas article in your magazine as heartwarming as this one." [This is insulting for two reasons: You're assuming you know more than the editor does, and you're implying that her magazine doesn't publish very heartwarming Christmas articles. Even if the latter is true, why bring it up?]

"I've always wanted to appear in your pages. With this article I believe I've finally fulfilled my fantasy." [All writers, even seasoned pros, feel—or should

feel—this way whenever they send out a query. But if you express such emotions on the page, you'll label yourself a gushy amateur and kill your chances. Instead, hope for the best, and hold your tongue.]

"Five other ideas that I'm sure will also interest you are the following . . . ." [Adding more ideas at the end of a detailed query sounds like an afterthought (which will hurt their chances); sounds like you're suddenly having second thoughts about your main idea (which is the last thing you want to do); or sounds like a desperate attempt to get something, anything, out of your query effort. Put all your effort into one idea per query. If you have other ideas, send other queries.]

"Please let me know when my article will appear so I can inform my friends and family." [I don't think this needs any explanation, do you?]

Egotistical

In an editorial meeting a few years ago, I proposed sending a writer to a Seniors golf tournament to hang out with the likes of Palmer, Nicklaus, Trevino, et al. My boss at the time raised an eyebrow and asked who I had in mind. Since we had been urged the month before to expand our own editorial responsibilities, I gulped and said, "Er, uh . . . me, actually."

My boss looked at me long and hard, and I'll never forget what she said. In front of everyone, she announced from across the room, "Who are *you*?" Her point, expressed rather crudely, was that if we send George Plimpton to observe a golf tournament, that's one thing. If we send George NoName, who cares? I argued that it was common practice at many publications for editors to report on various exotic goings-on ("our intrepid Travel editor strikes again . . ."). I also said that attaching an in-house name to a project makes the article seem more homey, full of more inside-scoop. Loyal readers build up trust for the magazines they read, and after a while the staffers on those publications become so familiar and reliable that the readers see them as quasi-friends or family members. My point was, you're more likely to read and believe a friend or family member's experience than a stranger's account. I lost the argument.

Nevertheless, my boss's instinct was more right than wrong. Unless you're well-known, few people want to read about you or your exploits. Americans are rabid about celebrities, but blasé about the man on the street. That's why a query that blatantly self-worships the writer is a journalistic turnoff. Hire a publicist to pitch us about your accomplishments instead. If we're interested, we'll assign a writer to profile you. That will free up time for you to query us on topics we *are* interested in.

Another turnoff is the "My wife and I just got back from a vacation in (pick anyplace), and we want to tell your readers about it." Slides included, of course. Wonderful. Just what we want to see—another slide show at the Bumpuses'.

This approach works best at newspapers, and even then, you usually have to hone in on a specific angle of your vacation for an editor to bite. Get away from you and your experiences, in other words, and focus on your destination and your activity. A good example of this is the *Los Angeles Times*'s Sunday Travel section's "Weekend Escape" column, which regularly profiles local family outings. The purpose of the section is to showcase a specific locale, describe what it offers, and itemize what a typical weekend for a family of three would set you back (a chart breaks down every expense). *That* interests me more than who the family is, why they went there, and what Susie and Johnny did when Grandma fell in the lake.

Reluctant

Just like in poker: If you hold a poor hand, don't tip off the other players. The less an editor knows about your shortcomings, the better. For example, if you have little or no writing credits, have written for only small publications, or have written about unrelated topics than the one you're proposing, *keep that fact to yourself.*

I get letters that say, almost boastfully, "Knowing I'm a writer, my family/friends/coworkers/teammates badgered me to share this experience with your readers, so here it is." An editor doesn't want to know that, if it wasn't for so-and-so, you wouldn't have bothered to get out of your BarcaLounger. We want writers who are banging on our door to get in, not ones whom we have to pull inside kicking and screaming.

One way to prevent this common slip is to avoid all references to how you got your idea in the first place. Once you open that Pandora's Box, the next thing you know you may blurt out something like, "I've never thought this essay was very good, but my mother loves it and asked me to send it to you."

Watch also for these other telltale suicidal phrases:

"Now, I admit . . ."
"I'll be honest with you . . ."

"I've never written before . . ."

"I've never done this before . . ."

"You may not believe this . . ."

"I've always wanted to try . . ."

"I realize this is not . . ."

Also avoid:

apologizing for anything

confessing to anything

pouring out your inner self

admitting a liability, then offering to disprove it

criticizing the publication

Loose-Lipped

Offering your potential manuscript "on spec," at least to many major newsstand magazines, is like handing them an amateur's business card. You're saying, in essence, "I don't have an ounce of confidence that this idea will get an assignment, so the only chance I have is to write it first and offer it to you with no obligation."

I used to do this all the time. It was an automatic phrase I tacked on to every one of my queries: "On spec, of course!" Egad, I could shoot myself today. (But why? I've already shot myself enough times.)

"But I'm a beginner," you say. "I've tried to get assignments and couldn't. The only sales I've made have been this way." Let me tell you a story. On August 13, 1977, Debbi Fields, a young chocolate-cookie entrepreneur, opened her first Mrs. Fields Chocolate Chippery in Palo Alto, California. Her husband, who had lent her the money for the risky venture, bet her she couldn't sell fifty dollars' worth by the end of her first day. By noon he was gloating; she hadn't sold a thing. Desperate, she picked up a tray of cookies, went outside, and literally handed them out for free to passersby on the sidewalk. By late afternoon he was glum; her shop was swamped. Since then she's made a lot more dough.

Everyone has heard success stories like this, of ambitious beginners who bucked the odds, risked it all, and succeeded. Freelancers, too, have prospered by handing out their articles "for free." So why am I so opposed to writers offering their articles this way despite success stories to the contrary?

Because Mrs. Fields's situation and yours are not the same.

Yes, I admit, the whole point of querying is to get your foot in the door by any means necessary. And yes, offering your article "on spec" can do that and will occasionally result in sales. And yes, I'm in favor of giving writers every break they can get. But Mrs. Fields's customers on that first day didn't care if she knew how to cook, which ingredients she used, how clean her kitchen was, or if her cookies were new. They just wanted to know how they tasted. Editors, unfortunately, aren't so easily pleased. We have a few more prerequisites we require before we'll reach into our wallet.

I'm willing to wager that offering your articles without the "S" word will help you more. If you cast your "on spec" line twenty times and get one editor to nibble, you may think you've done well. But if you don't use the "on spec" bait at all, you could hook maybe three editors—or, if only one, at least reeled her in after only five casts. Remember, editors prefer to deal with professionals (or with people they think are professionals). The dreaded "S" word—even in a promising query—tips us off that an amateur sent it. Since our careers hinge on the caliber of writers and successful projects we bring in and yours depends on winning our trust and confidence, the last thing you want to do is wave a red flag proclaiming "I am Beginner, hear me plead."

Here's another reason why you shouldn't give away the farm so quickly. A writer once sent me a story idea I liked, but his last sentence offered it to me "on spec." Since he was offering a free look, all the pressure was off me—and on him. He would now get all or nothing. If he hadn't offered me the piece "on spec" and I'd assigned the article to him, he would have gotten a check either way—the full fee or the kill fee if the piece didn't work out. Some kill fees alone can run into four figures.

Stubborn

Know when to say when. If you've been rejected again and again by the same editor at the same magazine, take the hint. Every editor I've talked to has experienced this unfortunate situation. Each of us knows a handful of writers who are clearly inappropriate for us (or their ideas always are) who just won't take no for an answer. They send in query after query after query—for years sometimes—and we keep sending them back.

My colleagues and I have racked our brains for the ideal solution to this problem. We don't want these writers to keep writing us and wasting their time, effort, and postage on a lost cause, and yet we don't want to insult them or discourage them by telling them the facts of publishing life.

I once asked a panel of magazine editors if any of them had experienced this situation. They all rolled their eyes and nodded. But when I asked them if they had ever tried to nip the problem in the bud by telling the writers, as gently as possible, "I'm sorry, but frankly we're never going to use your material. Please send your queries elsewhere," their laughter ceased. They all shook their heads.

I'm sure there are some insensitive editors out there who don't know or care about beginning writers' fragile self-esteem. I suspect, though, that the vast majority of editors don't have the heart to tell you the bad news. Maybe that's because they were writers themselves or still are. Unfortunately, neither one of these scenarios helps *you* very much. What, then, should you do if you suspect you're on an editor's blacklist? If you've sent more than six proposals to the same editor and gotten back nothing but form rejection letters, you have four options:

1. REVIEW YOUR MARKETING PROCEDURES

Have you been sending your letters to the wrong person? If so, go over my five-point plan in the previous chapter and reroute your future queries appropriately.

2. DROP THE EDITOR A NOTE

Politely say you've failed to pique her interest with your last several queries (include copies to refresh her memory) and ask for some constructive criticism. In all my years as an editor I have never received such an earnest note. I would not hesitate to reply to a writer who approached me so sincerely and professionally, and I suspect most other editors wouldn't either.

3. OUTLAST THE EDITOR

Wait until the editor who's been rejecting you switches assignments, moves up, or leaves (which they do often). Then resume your submissions to the person who takes her place (assuming that new person is still the right person to get your query).

4. DROP THE MAGAZINE FROM YOUR QUERY LIST PERMANENTLY

This advice applies to editors who have rejected every query letter with a form letter—and to those who don't respond to number two above. If an editor has ever jotted the least bit of encouragement ("nice try") on a rejection slip, however, keep her on your list.

Intrusive

One way to avoid the slush-pile, some writers believe, is to query the editor by phone. If they're going to get shot down, they figure, at least they'll get it over with in five minutes instead of the sometimes months it takes to get a rejection back. And if they get an OK, they can get started that day. Also, they'll avoid the sweat of having to crunch out dozens of queries each time out. Moreover, they'll endear themselves to editors by showing them that, (1) I'm a take-charge person who prefers to do things my way and not by the book; (2) I'm better at dealing with people face-to-face than on paper and am willing to prove it; (3) query letters are passé and a waste of time, so why should I do them just because all other freelancers (read sheep) do them; and (4) I've paid my dues and have earned the right to pick up the phone and call whomever whenever I damn well choose.

Please don't cold-call an editor. Ever. Otherwise you come across as a prime-time phone huckster who demands a decision on his merchandise during *Monday Night Football*. The telephone is the tool of telemarketers, not writers. An editor needs to see how you write, not how you talk. Even if an editor likes your oral pitch, she's still going to need a query letter specifying the details. We've got enough problems than to have to explain why your proposal on "beard detangling" isn't for us. Sometimes we *can't* explain the reason. Sometimes we can but don't want to get into a drawn-out debate about it, which many of these calls evolve into. And, from vast experience, I know which question will punctuate the end of every such call: "Well then, what *are* you looking for?" Whoa. That's like asking how many angels can dance on the head of a pin. It is the question of the ages. It has hung over the head of every newspaper, magazine, and book publisher since the invention of the printing press. It is not a question, therefore, to blithely ask an editor. The best answer to that I've ever come up with is: "I'll tell you what we're looking for. We're looking for an idea different from the one you proposed. Read the magazine."

But, you say, not all writer-editor calls are queries. OK, let's look at them:

"What if I just want to introduce myself?" [That's what query letters are for. Chances are your call will catch the editor at an inappropriate time or

when she's not in the mood, either one of which could sour her initial impression of you.]

"What if I've been invited to join a press junket that leaves next week, and I need a confirmed assignment from an editor before I can go?" [Editors don't appreciate having guns held to their heads. Plan your stories to meet the publications' deadlines, not your own.]

"What if I was given the OK to call you by another staff editor?" [Even though another staff editor may have given you the "OK," you didn't get it from the editor you're going to approach. So don't call; instead, write a query and mention that so-and-so referred you.]

"What if I want to run some ideas by you to see if any are worth an official query later—a "pre-query," in other words?" [A lot of writers try this, but it's a sneaky way around procedure and will backfire. It labels you as lazy instead of resourceful.]

"What if I've already sold something to you before?" [Actually, this is the only time it's OK to approach an editor by phone. Once you've written for someone once or twice, she will be more receptive to your call. Not very receptive, just more.]

But the main reason why you should never call an editor with a query idea is this: Even if I have the time and interest, which I probably won't, would you honestly want your cherished concept to hinge on one thirty-second snap judgment from someone who's harried and disgruntled?

But don't query letters get only thirty seconds of attention? Aren't they also decided mostly by snap judgments by frazzled editors? Yes, but the difference is, most queries are read in one sitting when the editor has set aside time for them. We have to get into the proper (if there is one) mind-set for reading them. As I've said before, wading through queries is not fun. Once we're into the task, though, we're into it totally and take it seriously. That's a much better atmosphere for your idea, trust me, than when I'm in the middle of a deadline, on my lunch hour, or walking out the door.

Inappropriate

Try to attach clips similar in style or subject matter to the idea you're proposing. Example: If you're pitching a 2,000-word profile of Dallas Cowboys' quarterback Troy Aikman, include the profile you did of Denver Broncos' quarterback John Elway—even if it's a couple of years old—not the latest piece you did on entertaining the in-laws. You want to attach clips that are related as closely as possible to your idea so the editor can see how you handle that particular genre or style. In the Aikman example, any pieces you've done on sports, football, quarterbacks, Dallas Cowboys, Dallas, or even Texas would be helpful.

Even experienced writers with lots of clips occasionally lose out on assignments this way, figuring if they throw in the latest piece they sold, its freshness will impress the editor more. Maybe. But if it's a close call between assigning your idea and another writer's idea, and the other writer's clips are more tailored to his presentation and give a better preview of how his piece will look and read, you may lose the gig.

But can't you judge my writing from whatever clips I enclose? Yes and no. I assign and edit the "MM Interview" each issue. Writing a Q&A is a difficult, unique, and underrated craft, and it takes a special kind of writer to pull it off. You may be a wonderful essayist or consumer reporter or travel writer, as your clips attest, but I would have serious misgivings assigning you a Q&A with Madonna based on an essay, consumer article, or travel article. And I bet an Essay editor, Consumer editor, or Travel editor would have the same qualms about assigning one of their articles if you show her only Q&A clips.

What if you don't have any similar clips? In that case, just attach the best you have. If you have no clips whatsoever, that's fine, too. Just don't call attention to it.

Careless

The final sin to steer clear of is making a slip of the pen that, at first glance, may read pleasantly but, on closer inspection, bares your most severe liability—in twenty-point type.

Here's what just a few unfortunate writers inadvertently revealed to me:

"This is the first time I've written to a magazine." [Might as well just stamp AMATEUR across the top of your letter.]

"Most of my writing is for automotive trade magazines." [If your idea is about automobiles, fine. If it's not, this tells the editor you may be venturing out of your league.]

"I realize this is rather vague and difficult for you or your staff to evaluate as to interest and noteworthiness, but I sincerely believe I can contribute to your publication with many human-interest stories." [The writer never did get around to proposing an idea.]

"My one published credit is enclosed." [This writer spoiled a perfectly good query letter by saying that. Never broadcast that you're starting out.]

"I enclose a sample of my writing . . . not exactly the same sort of writing I propose doing for you, but you're entitled to see something." [If you don't have any appropriate clips to show an editor, say nothing and enclose nothing. By all means, don't do and say what this writer did.]

"Please send me your list of topics to be covered next year." [A lot of publications haven't finalized (or even conceptualized) what they're going to publish the following year. And that's just the major features. As for all the departmental fillers and columns, who knows? Don't worry that you might come up with something we're already working on; the odds are low that that will happen, and if it does, try somewhere else.]

And my three personal favorites:

"I have written a 20,000-word article on the drop-kick. It is from my book's chapter on kicking."

"I'm sending you this article on a brothel in northern Nevada, although it may not be suitable for your magazine."

"I promise you the finished article will be much more interesting than this proposal."

Don't make the same mistakes! The best way to avoid these gaffes is, of course, don't commit them in the first place. The next best way is to proofread your queries carefully before sending them out.

Those are the Ten Query Sins. To show you how all ten mistakes would look together in one letter, I created a hypothetical Poor Query Letter (incorporating all Ten Query Sins and misusing all Ten Query Commandments) on the next page.

Poor Article Query Letter

1.

> Robert Williams
> Editor-in-Chief
> Travelcade Magazine
> 123 Main Street
> New York, NY 12345
> Dear Bob,

2.

> Rio de Janeiro is a wonderland of travel experiences that should not be missed by travelers young or old. It's the place to go for sun and fun, and not only that—it's replete with a samba beat!

3. 4. & 5.

> For your readers who have not yet been there, I would like to recount a recent trip my wife and I took to the Brazilian vacation spot. We spent a long time planning this vacation—we pored over dozens of travel brochures and talked to many tour operators and travel agents. Traveling to a foreign country can be hazardous in more ways than one, so it's crucial to choose an operator who is a specialist in the locale you're visiting. We chose an outfit called Rio Bravo because we liked the manager and everyone seemed very nice and knowledgeable. And their prices were good, too. Another thing we had to take into account before we went was our age—we're not spring chickens anymore. I'm 66 and my wife is 62; I have a cataract in one eye and had a hip replacement five years ago and my wife suffers from emphysema. We wanted a vacation that was fun and adventuresome, but not too much, if you know what I mean. After we told all our

1. UNPROFESSIONAL

This writer automatically sent his query letter to the top name on the magazine's masthead, not realizing that editors-in-chief never read query letters. On top of that, he addressed him as "Bob," which you can bet "Bob" did not appreciate, and forgot to include an SASE.

2. DULL

The lead is as important to a query letter as it is to an article. This one is bland and cliché-ridden. Most editors wouldn't read further. All this writer's effort in composing his letter, therefore, would have been in vain.

3. EGOTISTICAL

Readers want to read about a vacation locale, not about *your* vacation. There's a big difference. The more you infuse yourself into your queries, the less interest you'll generate.

4. WORDY

Don't be the Energizer Writer ("he keeps going and going . . ."). This one segues into minutiae and gets lost in no-man's-land. Imagine how the article would read!

5. RELUCTANT

Hey, don't do anything your friends have to talk you into doing—and certainly don't tell that to an editor!

friends about our Rio trip, they told us we described it so well, they felt like signing up for a trip themselves. So, with their insistence, I wrote this up and sent it in. But I digress. Below are the topics I would be happy to write for you:

6. 7. 8. & 9.

Corcovado (the giant Christ statue—breathtaking!)
Sugar Loaf (the cable car that James Bond fought on!)
Shopping for gems (we'll sample Copacabana's finest emporiums!)
Girl-watching (are the bikinis really that tiny—yes!)
Carnaval (still the greatest show on earth!)

10.

Just let us know which of the following stories you're interested in, and we'll send 'em out ASAP! (By the way, I'd also like to know how much you pay for such articles and how soon you pay after you buy them.)

11. 12. & 13.

Being two retirees, we have more than a few years of traveling behind us and can give this trip an "older generational" perspective that your younger readers would, we're sure, be interested in. After all, they'll all be old one day, too. (And many older people still travel as we do.) So, would you like to see 5,000 words on the hottest city in South America? I know that's a lot of words, but you'll be doing your readers a disservice in anything less—there's just so much to tell! We could have any one of these pieces on your desk in a week.

6. UNCREATIVE

The writer not only buries his idea(s) too far into the letter, but does nothing to herald them (no catchy head and subhead) once we dig them up.

7. OLD

These ideas are old-fashioned, gushy, and corny, which are a dead giveaway to what the finished piece will look like.

8. SKETCHY

As written, these hooks wouldn't appeal to the most desperate editor. They give no details, no color, no angle to the stories.

9. UNFOCUSED

Although the writer offers different aspects of Rio, he stops well short of providing a unique insight on any of them. We've all seen stories about Carnaval. Instead, why not narrow that further by profiling a particular samba school? Or delve into one school's parade floats (it's meaning, theme, designer, cost, participants, etc.)?

10. PRESUMPTUOUS

Don't be so quick to close the sale or count your money; that'll spook an editor faster than a Rupert Murdoch takeover bid.

11. UNSUITABLE

Always target your idea to the right magazine. This writer admits the idea isn't right for the publication, but sends it in anyway! Don't try to fit a square peg into a round hole.

14.

> On speculation, of course!

15. 16. & 17.

> I must confess to you that I've never written a travel article before, but I was a technical writer for thirty-six years and would love to give it a try. This is my tenth attempt at selling an idea to you, by the way—you sure are a tough nut to crack—but I'm not a quitter and am sure this one will do the trick!

18.

> Sincerely,
> John Jones
> 123 Maple Drive
> Anytown, CA 90000
> 213-555-9000
>
> Enclosures:
> Resume
> Technical manual
> [no SASE]

12. UNREALISTIC

Don't show your naiveté by assuming a small idea should be done in 5,000 words or a big idea can be done in 1,500—or any article can be brought in in one week.

13. ONE-DIMENSIONAL

The writer offers no extras or options to further lure an indecisive editor (i.e., sidebars, suggestions on where else it could fit into the magazine, other ways to do it, etc.).

14. LOOSE-LIPPED

The "S" word tips an editor off that you're a beginner. Never broach this subject; let the editor do that.

15. CARELESS

How such horrors slip into queries is beyond me. Proofread your letters to catch such clunkers!

16. UNACCREDITED

Not only is the writer unqualified to write this piece, but he announces it to the whole world. Keep your shortcomings to yourself.

17. STUBBORN

If you've been rejected again and again by the same editor, take the hint. She ain't gonna call.

18. INAPPROPRIATE

Resumes tell editors nothing. We want to know how you write, not where you've worked or went to school. This writer should have attached a travel clip instead of a technical-writing sample because that matches the kind of writing he's proposing.

19. & 20.

> P.S.: On second thought, maybe Rio's been done to death. If so, maybe you'd be interested in an article about a cruise to the Bahamas instead? I'll call you in a couple of weeks to follow-up.

19. DISPASSIONATE

Say what? What happened to Rio? This isn't the time or place to change your mind just to sneak in one more pitch.

20. INTRUSIVE

Never follow-up a query with a phone call—certainly not for this reason. The only reason to contact an editor again would be if you don't hear back for a month or two. And then send a follow-up letter.

Questions & Answers

Q: You assert that editors rarely steal ideas, but I remain unconvinced. If you get a great idea from a bad writer, what's to stop you from telling him, "No thanks," and assigning it to a writer you like?

A: Just a nasty lawsuit, hefty damages, and grievous publicity. Art Buchwald sued Paramount for doing just that to his story idea that begat Eddie Murphy's *Coming to America* (for which he was awarded $150,000 in 1992). Television and movie studios have to pay and credit writers for story ideas. Publications aren't nearly as generous with bylines, but most do pay idea fees.

I once faced a sticky situation regarding an idea. I liked a writer's query very much but surmised from her clips, style, and background that she wasn't the right writer for the story she wanted to do. It just so happened, however, that we had been keeping a top-name writer under wraps for precisely this kind of delicate and offbeat project. Since she had introduced the idea to us and since we wanted to assign it—but not to her—we owed her compensation. So far so good. Editors are paid—and have the right—to match who they feel are the best writers for each concept.

So I called the writer, explained why I didn't have the confidence to assign this particular project to her, apprised her of our plans vis-à-vis the other writer, and offered her an idea fee. She went ballistic, refused the fee, and threatened to sue if we used her idea. We said, in effect, "Fine, then don't take the money," and went ahead and assigned it to the second writer. Was this theft?

No, and I'll tell you why. She had every right to be angry and even to refuse the fee, but once she turned the money down she had no right to deny us the idea, too. She was saying, in essence, to each magazine she sent it to: "If you don't assign it to me, you can't assign it to anybody else *from this day forward*." That's information blackmail. Ideas can't be copyrighted. (For those of you who side with the writer, you'll be pleased to know that the resulting article by the "top-name" writer bombed. It was killed to put it, and all of us, out of misery.)

Q: The only clips I have might offend the magazine I want to query to. Should I attach them?

A: When I started out writing, the first sales I made were to men's magazines. When I tried later to branch out to general-interest publications, those clips posed a problem. I asked an editor at a writing seminar what I should do, and he advised me not to include them. "But they're good pieces," I protested. "They show off my style; they're not smut." He shook his head. "They could still hurt you more than help you." He was probably right because I eventually broke into other markets by not sending in those writing samples. I would advise the same to you: Don't include clips that are grossly (in more ways than one) different from the market you're pitching.

Q: Do resume queries (letters that outline your qualifications and state you're seeking assignments but don't propose an idea) ever work?

A: Rarely. We get some of these, and most are tossed or sent back. On a few occasions, however, when the clips and background are impressive, I put the material into my "Good Writers" file to consider for possible future assignments. But the last time I looked, those letters still languish there. If an editor needs something assigned fast, he'll usually go to somebody he knows and trusts before he scrapes the bottom of his files. You'll have a better shot of getting an assignment if your query letter includes an article idea.

If you want to try the resume-query route, though, at least portray your-self as a specialist by narrowing your qualifications and background to one particular subject matter so the editor will remember you as "that real sharp bicycling writer." If you present yourself as just another general-interest writer, you may disappear into the drawer.

CHAPTER FIVE

The Nonfiction Book Query and Proposal

"One man is as good as another until he has written a book."
William Faulkner

For those of you just joining us from the article-query chapters, let me warn you before you proceed: The task of writing a query just got, shall we say, more challenging. If you thought squeezing a 3,000-word article concept into one page was tough, you're now going to learn what it takes to summarize a 50,000- or a 100,000-word project into a query letter.

As for how you're supposed to also get a favorable response to that letter, know this: Fewer books are published than newspaper and magazine articles. Books are bigger projects than articles, cost more money, and stand to leave a larger crater in an organization should they bomb. Plus, authors have to have substantially developed their projects by the initial query stage, whereas newspaper and magazine writers merely have to have fleshed out an idea at that juncture. Oh, and one more thing: Most agents and book editors require *two* sales presentations—a query and a proposal—before they'll give you the go-ahead.

Still with me? Ah, just what I like to see—stout-hearted lads and lasses. Now that you've passed the first test of will, I have some good news for you. Any writer can write a nonfiction book. Any writer. That's because every nonfiction book ever published was written by an expert—health experts, winning-at-blackjack experts, weight-loss experts, success experts, investment-planning experts, sex experts—even query-writing experts.

What—you say you're not an expert? Everyone's an expert at something—even you. All it takes to be an "expert" is to know a little bit more about something than most people. Unless you've lived in a cave all your life, you're bound to qualify as an expert at something. (And if you *have* lived in a cave all your life, you're an expert at that.)

Do you know how to change the oil and spark plugs in your car? You may have the makings for a how-to-extend-your-car's-life guide. Have you ever been conned or burglarized? You've got the makings of a how-not-to-get-ripped-off book. Do you have a green thumb even though you live in a high-rise apartment? Hundreds of thousands of other apartment-dwellers would love to read your *How to Grow Anything From the Sixteenth Floor* book. Are you pregnant? Record a journal and call it *My First Nine Months* by Baby Jennie. I'd read it.

As I was writing this chapter, I scanned the bestseller list to see what the latest "experts" were writing about. I found the following: Are you into baseball memorabilia? David Halberstam was (result: *October 1964*). Did your mother die recently? Hope Edelman's did (result: *Motherless Daughters*). Have you ever had a near-death experience? Betty J. Eadie did (result: *Embraced by the Light*). Do you live in a small town? Bailey White does (result: *Mama Makes Up Her Mind*). Have you ever worked for someone famous? Rosie Daley is Oprah Winfrey's cook (result: *In the Kitchen with Rosie*). Do you prescribe medicine? Psychiatrist Peter D. Kramer does (result: *Listening to Prozac*). Has life taught you anything? H. Jackson Brown, Jr., thinks so (result: *Life's Little Instruction Book*). I could go on, which unfortunately I have. You're an expert at whatever you know or can do. You're an expert at whatever or whoever interests you. You're an expert at whatever's happened to you in your life. Says who? Says *you*—and don't let anybody tell you differently.

The point is, deciding *what* to write is the easy part. Getting an agent or an editor to consider taking it on is the hard part. To do that, you first need to get their attention (via a query letter) and then you need to get their commitment (via a proposal). Let's see how to do each one separately.

The Query

Good news! Remember when I said agents and editors require both a query and a proposal before they'll say OK? Well, that extra work can also work in your favor. Sure, your task has been doubled, but it also means you now get two chances, not just one, to sell your project. Once your query evokes the magic words, "Yes, I want to see more," you've just jumped out of the slush-pile. The agent or the editor now knows your name and letterhead, is anticipating your proposal, is ready and willing to deal with you one-on-one. What's more, she's obligated herself; she owes you a more thorough read than if you'd just sent in the whole package unsolicited.

Agents and editors prefer this two-step arrangement, too. It allows them more time and opportunities to judge you and your project than if they only had one pass at the material. They know saying "yes" to your query only means they've agreed to see your proposal, not your entire book. They're not signing you on as a client or buying your book. There's less pressure on you, too. Your whole book doesn't rest on your one query, like an article does. You don't have to close the sale; you just have to whet her appetite. She doesn't have to buy or sign a contract if she likes it, she just has to be willing to see more.

With a few differences and additional advice noted below, all Ten Query Commandments still apply to book queries. They must be:

1. PROFESSIONAL

Make sure your letter is neat, error-free, no longer than a page-and-a-half, accompanied by an SASE, and addressed to the right agent or editor.

Notice I said "addressed to the right agent *or* editor." One of the challenges with book queries is that there is another player involved besides the editor—the agent, which raises the question: Whom do you query first—an agency or a publisher? Some writers think approaching a publisher is better. That's because if you get an offer from a publisher, all the power reverts to you. Virtually every agent who deals with your kind of book will be at your mercy. What agent would not want to represent a writer waving a book contract? It's the perfect win-win situation: You get an instant agent and someone else to do the negotiating; the agent avoids having to schlep the book around and still gets her fee.

Unfortunately, there's one serious drawback to this method: The publishing industry is moving farther and farther away from allowing writers to submit material by themselves. Most publishers today prefer that agents screen your idea, material, and qualifications first. According to agent Jeff Herman in his book, *Insider's Guide to Book Editors, Publishers and Literary Agents*: "Most major publishing houses have policies that prevent them from even considering unagented/unsolicited submissions."

That's why I always advise authors to query agents before approaching publishers. An agent has many potential "clients" to pitch your book to; an acquiring editor at a publishing house has just one. If you land an agent first, her representation will generate any number of good things: Her submission at each publishing house will bypass the slush-pile. It will go to the right editor. It will arrive in its own special folder, cover letter, and Good House-keeping Seal of Approval from the agency. It will signify that your query has been prescreened and selected from among hundreds of lesser-qualified submissions. It will put the agent's and agency's reputation on the line. It will place an eager promoter in your corner who can generate "buzz" for your book before anyone has seen it and, if you're lucky, maybe even set up an auction for it between several bidding publishers. And it will give you security knowing the agent is an expert negotiator, bargainer, and hardball player who knows how to throw heat and has a vested interest in getting you—and herself—the best deal.

How do you know which agent and agency to approach? The quickest way is to scan your local bookstore for books similar to your idea. Look in the acknowledgments section of these books. Writers often thank their agent and/or book editor here. If an agency's name is mentioned along with the agent's, query the agent there and state that the reason you're contacting her is because the book you're writing is similar to (name of book) that she recently sold to (name of publisher).

If the book's "Acknowledgments" page mentions the agent's name but not her agency, or just thanks a bunch of people, one of whom *could be* the agent, look up the name(s) in the alphabetical index in *The Literary Market-place* (available at your local library). If one of the names is a literary agent, the index will link her to her agency. If the author didn't thank his or her agent or editor in the "acknowledgments" page, call the publisher and ask for the publicity or subsidiary rights department. Ask whoever answers for the name of the agency that represents the author of that book. Call the agency and ask which agent represents that author.

A longer but still-effective way is to peruse the "Book Publishers" chapter in the current *Writer's Market* for names and addresses of publishers that publish the kind of book you're proposing. Request free catalogs from these publishers and comb them for books similar to your concept. Most catalogs identify the agencies and/or agents affiliated with each of their listed books. Call the agencies associated with these books and ask for the name of the agent who represented the book's author. Then query the agent in the manner described above.

Since most unpublished writers aren't this thorough, their letters will usually wind up in an agency's or editor's slush-pile and be read by editorial assistants. Yours, on the other hand, will arrive all by itself on the appropriate agent's or editor's desk, customized to her individual interests and expertise.

2. NEW

Study the competition to ensure that your book differs significantly from what's out there. Let's say your book is about how men and women differ from each other. One best-seller last year was *Men Are From Mars: Women Are From Venus* by John Gray, Ph.D. To ensure your idea stands apart from Gray's and the clones that followed *his* success, study these books and see what they covered and didn't cover. Then come up with an angle that breaks new ground—while still addressing the same overall theme.

Next come up with a great title, like Gray's, that will raise eyebrows. If you're not good at titles, browse a bookshop and analyze the best-selling nonfiction titles (note I said "best-selling"; they often sport the best ones)—even those unrelated to your book's subject matter. What words, phrases, and elements make those titles and subtitles so tantalizing? The more you study them, the more the secrets of good titles will become apparent to you. When you feel you're ready to give it a try, create a title and subtitle for your book, stamp them right up front in your letter, and highlight them by boldfacing, capitalizing, and centering them.

3. PROVOCATIVE

As with magazine queries, open with a bang. You want to get the reader's attention—get her out of her "skim-and-reject default mode." So hit her between the eyes with a two-by-four—your lead—and make her say, "Hmm, this one might be interesting."

If your book's opening paragraph is scintillating (and it should be), consider opening with that. Or use one of your favorite anecdotes from the book. Or reveal a startling statistic that illustrates why your book must be told. In *The Awful Truth About Publishing*, author John Boswell recalls two classic introductions. Jackie Sorensen, who created the aerobic-dancing movement, pitched her first book with this opening sentence: "Aerobic dancing is a complete physical-fitness program that whispers exercise and shouts fun." Astronaut Pete Conrad blasted his book off this way: "I did not sleep very well the night before I went to the moon." Writer Caroline Bird suggested this one to me: "I'm an ex-girlfriend of O.J. Simpson and am willing to tell all." Only a brain-dead agent or editor would quit reading after such openings.

Another way is to start off the body of your letter with a one-sentence description of your book, called a "handle" or "hook":

> "If I had to describe my book in one sentence, I would say it's a cross between *The One-Minute Manager* and *How to Make Love All Night Long*—or *The 1990s Guide to Sex Time-Management*"

or

> "If I had to describe my book in one sentence, I would call it *Father Knows Best* meets *The Silence of the Lambs*—or *Memoirs of My Serial-Killer Dad*"

In the *New York Times Book Review*, Judith Hooper and Dick Teresi wrote that the best handle they ever saw was: "This is a new book by Stephen King." Unfortunately, this handle works for very few authors.

4. CREATIVE

The same advice holds true here as it does with article queries: Don't be afraid to break from the standard letter format. You want your letter to visually stand out—even if just a little—from your competitors. So experiment with indented, justified, or boxed paragraphs; variable margins; italic, boldface, or underlined subheads; numbered or bulleted lists; etc. As with everything, however, don't overdo it or do it just because you can. Use each element only when it's appropriate.

5. FOCUSED

Just because a book's length is much longer than a magazine article's doesn't mean your topic can be broader and roomier than a magazine piece. Most nonfiction books, like magazine assignments, highlight only one small corner of the whole picture. For example, a pocket guide called *How to Win at Tennis* sounds, on the surface, like it would appeal to a general audience. In actuality it's amorphous; it doesn't say anything, at least nothing very new or useful. *How to Win at Tennis After Forty* is better because it targets a specific audience. Better still would be *Fifty Ways to Improve Your Tennis Serve After Forty*. Now *that* would carve out a niche all your own and a following whose specific needs are being met.

The subject matter of one of last year's blockbusters, *The Hot Zone*, was killer viruses. But the author didn't just publish a general overview of mean microbes. To focus his topic and make his account read more like a story, he concentrated on the most feared virus in the world, e-bola, and—narrowing his theme even further—on the most dangerous near-outbreak in recent history in Reston, Virginia.

Another book, which was made into a recent hit movie, was *The Lost Moon*. Its theme was the U.S. space program, the Apollo missions, and America's frantic race to the moon in the sixties and seventies. But what made the book a real page-turner was not the broad subject but the author's focus on one specific moon mission—the ill-fated Apollo 13 mission that nearly ended in disaster.

6. CUSTOMIZED

Send your queries only to those agents, agencies, and publishers who handle the same subject matter as your book. This sounds silly to point out, but many writers send poems to magazines that never publish poetry, or crossword-puzzle book queries to detective-mystery publishers. Research the agents, agencies, and publishing houses beforehand to make sure they handle the kind of book you're proposing.

7. MULTIFACETED

If your idea can't be physically produced the normal way (i.e., it won't fit the standard book format and/or will require unusual elements like large print, pop-ups, cut-outs, CD-ROMs, cassettes, etc.), present examples of what you intend to do or offer optional formats to show different ways it could be done. Never assume an agent or editor will think of these options. Fortunately for me, the editor and publisher of this book did. They juggled several different ways of laying it out and designing it, finally agreeing on a large-format size to ensure enough space for the annotated sample letters it would contain. If I had suggested the large-format size for this book as an option early on (which I didn't), I may have eased the initial brainstorming process considerably—or, if they had been on the fence, clinched the sale.

8. REALISTIC

A low-key approach is always better than a hard sell. Your professionalism is even more crucial to an agent or a book editor than it is to a magazine or a newspaper editor because so much more rests on a book project than on an article assignment. I know the impulse is to get the reader so excited in your concept that she'll grab the phone and call you immediately. But be careful not to promise too much just to get someone's attention or to set goals beyond your capabilities. And in your writing, dispense with the exclamation points. Ideally, your idea should do all the talking. If you don't think your idea is sufficient to sell anyone, then maybe it's time to rethink your book.

9. ACCREDITED

Present your writing credits and describe your expertise, reputation, credentials, and/or access to the subject or subject matter you're proposing: "My five years as a lifeguard, my volunteer work with the Coast Guard, and my love of channel swimming qualify me to write *Ocean Swimming Safety.* . . ." Skip any part of your background that is irrelevant to your idea: "I also have a degree in economics and currently work as a vice president at a local bank."

10. CONCLUSIVE

Show me you're the best writer to take on this project and you care the most about it. Don't just say, "I really, really want to write this book." Show me why you're willing to devote two years to this project. I want to feel what's in your head, in your gut, in your heart. It's like the difference between two actors auditioning for a part that involves an emotional scene. The first actor shrieks and lunges and beats his chest and sobs and sinks to the floor in a blubbering heap. The second actor subtly stiffens as the shock and rage build rapidly within him—his facial defenses giving nothing away. He starts to cross the room, takes two unsure steps, then finally lets it all out—with a single teardrop. You don't believe the first actor; you'll never forget the second one. Al Pacino as Michael Corleone learning his brother Fredo is the traitor. Kirk Douglas as a crucified Spartacus seeing his wife and child for the last time. Don't worry about being too subtle. If you're passionate about your project, your determination and its significance will be evident in your words.

Once again, to show you how all ten principles would look together in one letter, I created a hypothetical Ideal Nonfiction Book Query on the next page. I chose not to diagram a hypothetical Poor Nonfiction Book Query because the most common book-query Sins, and the advice I would give on how to prevent them, are virtually the same as those discussed in the article-query chapter. The book-query Commandments, on the other hand, have a few new areas to explore.

Ideal Nonfiction Book Query Letter

1.

> Harold Murphy
> Murphy Literary Agency
> 555 Times Square
> New York, NY 11111
> Dear Mr. Murphy:

2.

> ### The Celestial Conspiracy
> The shocking behind-the-scenes revelation:
> Are angels really aliens?

3.

> Several years ago, the popularity of angels suddenly and inexplicably soared across America, garnering miraculous blessings for those publishers whose clairvoyance foretold that their books would rise to the top of the bestseller lists. Books such as *Where Angels Walk*, *Where Miracles Happen*, *A Gathering of Angels*, *The Angels Within Us*, *An Angel to Watch Over Me*, and *Angel Letters* reaped more than 1 million sales.
>
> Was it just a coincidence that at the same time, a tenfold increase in UFO sightings and abductions occurred around the world? These phenomena prompted a similarly unexplained wave of articles, books, and movies—from *Close Encounters of the Third Kind* to *Communion* to *Fire in the Sky* to *Abduction* to Steven Spielberg's rumored new blockbuster, *Project X*.
>
> What do these two cultish trends have in common? *The Celestial Conspiracy* will prove that angels and aliens not only exist, *they are one and the same*.

1. PROFESSIONAL

The writer not only narrowed his submission to the right agent but he explained why that agent was right for his project (see the fifth box). Any agent or editor would appreciate this amount of in-depth research and personalization.

2. NEW

By showcasing your book's catchy title and subhead quickly and conspicuously, as this writer did, you'll pull the reader in at once.

3. PROVOCATIVE

After catching the reader's eye with his title, this writer drew him in with his lead. Whatever you say in your lead, make it a doozy. This one certainly is.

4. & 5.

I analyzed and compared more than 150 global "incidents" of angel and UFO sightings during the past few years and uncovered these astonishing findings:

Eighty-five percent of all "angel" entities sighted contained striking similarities to alien beings (i.e., at least ten out of the fifteen official alien characteristics that distinguish extraterrestial life forms, as designated by the Center for UFO Studies) and 96 percent of all "aliens" exhibited remarkable likenesses and behavior to that of angels (as described by eyewitnesses and from accounts taken from the Bible). My book's conclusion: There are three types of aliens—(1) harmless and curious sightseers, (2) sinister and rapacious abductors, and (3) comforting and "divine" guardians—a.k.a. "angels."

6. & 1.

Timely, definitive, shocking. My book is ideal for you because its subject matter mirrors some of your most successful clients' projects, namely Bill Smith's *Alien Storm* and Wilma Johnson's *Devils Among Us*. I notice you also sell many books to Simon & Schuster. My book could fit nicely into their recently launched "Inquiry" line of new-wave investigative works on stories that are, as the publisher says, "on the razor's edge of journalism."

8. & 10.

The Celestial Conspiracy is the result of five-and-a-half years of extraordinary research, perseverance, and access to never-before-seen top-secret information from government UFO files, scientific paranormal material, church documents, and historical data ranging from CIA transcriptions to the *Dead*

4. CREATIVE

It always helps to set off one section of your letter in a special way to catch the reader's eye and draw him in farther. This writer indented and justified a portion of one paragraph and highlighted it with italics. Then he wisely turned off the charm the rest of the way. He'd achieved his objective. Too much razzle-dazzle can sometimes backfire.

5. FOCUSED

There are dozens of books about angels and undoubtedly more about aliens, but this writer found an angle all his own. Is there any better way to eliminate your competition?

6. CUSTOMIZED

If an agent or an editor receives a letter researched and targeted this precisely, as this one is, and that person doesn't sit up and take notice, then by sheer bad luck you've sent it to a moron.

7. MULTIFACETED

Unlike magazine articles, which can be written, structured, and designed in myriad ways and accompanied by an assortment of elements, most books are usually done the same old way. Since this particular book won't require an unconventional format or unusual elements, this Commandment doesn't apply here.

Sea Scrolls. My findings will shatter the beliefs and faith of millions of people. Those who doubted will forever believe. Those who believed will forever doubt. And those who read it will never forget.

9.

For your information, I hold a Ph.D. from Harvard in Paranormal Studies and an M.A. from Berkeley in Religious History. I am currently the Science Editor of *Omni* and chair the award-winning *Astronomy Forum* weekly program on National Public Radio. I am a winner of the George Polk Memorial Award for Journalism and the author of five other books on extraterrestial and out-of-body phenomena.

1.

Enclosed are tear sheets from reviews of my two most recent books. I look forward to hearing from you.

Sincerely,

John Jones
123 Maple Drive
Anytown, CA 90000
213-555-7766

Enclosure:
Book reviews
SASE

8. REALISTIC

Any idea—especially one as wacky as this—had better instill confidence that you can deliver what you're proposing and that your research and conclusions are sound. This writer did a good job of laying a strong framework for his claims.

9. ACCREDITED

All qualifications were pertinent, impressive, and matter-of-fact. No extraneous information, no puffed-up self-praise. This said volumes, whereas a voluminous bio would have said little.

10. CONCLUSIVE

It takes a certain skill to be subtle, yet passionate. Understated, yet exuberant. The last three sentences in this box pulled it off.

Sample Letters

Dear Lisa,

As you know, I've been organizing material for a book about my family and the ranch Margaret and I own here in Montana. Although I've used this area before, as the setting for a novel and to ground various essays and short stories, I haven't yet explored my own life as it has been woven into the fabric of my family's century-long experience here. It has been, however, my great good fortune to come from people who created not only a place to live but a homeplace, that condition of the heart which for most of us is as needed and necessary as breath.

I want to stress up front that I am not suggesting another homesteading saga or ranching epic, nor am I interested in writing a reminiscence of better days gone by in some idyllic but lost place. We don't listen to the hog report, and I don't expect readers to wallow through the muck of daily farm routines. We do still raise cattle here, though, and face the same difficulties of weather and topography that my great-grandparents had to endure. Our ranch has not been easy to own; it has always been a break-even deal at best, and it has completely broken some of us. But there is, in the blend of work and blood, of promise and loss, a continuity and an enduring love for the land itself which has touched and shaped each generation, and that has to do with what we mean when we talk about the power of place and the sacredness of home.

I propose to write the memoir of an American family place in Montana, from 1880 to the present. Told from the vantage point of the fifth generation, *In These Hills* is the story of a people who settled along the Jackson Creek drainage in the hope that land could set them free. It is an attempt, as well, to recapture the spirit of each succeeding generation's existence here and to articulate how those people are still here, as inseparable from the land they worked and the houses and barns they built as my life has been inseparable from theirs. Their legacy is more than an assortment of corrals, cattle receipts, and story fragments. What has happened in this place carries forward a message and a metaphor about a people and a way of life in America which may soon pass from this world forever.

In These Hills is also about my own life in this country and the slow path of discovery which has led me to some understanding of my blood people and our neighbors by locating myself in the countryside they inhabited and by continuing the enterprises they shared. When I returned in the mid-seventies, after years away at college and at war, I took on the job of reviving the ranch into a working operation. In the years that followed, I have been able to return through the physical place to the interior landscapes of my childhood, and with the eyes of a man rediscover the place as it was as well as the boy I had been. As I restored the ranch, I was somehow restored too. The more I engaged in the work here, the more I learned about the men and women in my family and how they had made this place what it was; and the more

I learned about them, the more I discovered about the man I would become.

I am reminded during haying, for example, of how, after the fields had been cleared of trees and rocks, after brush fires had burned for weeks and the stumps had been shot free with black powder, my great-grandfather and his twelve-year-old son pressed the timothy seed of their first crop into the black earth of our meadows by rolling a hollow log around and around the fields by hand. And, as each time I have mowed the hay they planted, I have been reminded of how it was planted, of the poverty and determination, the strength and fatigue, the sweat and hope that accompanied its planting. And I experience at such times a sweet if fleeting sense of connection with them and with something larger than myself that nonetheless includes me, as if, after the years of my own labor in those fields, pushing that log has come to be part of my own life.

Perhaps because no one in my family was educated beyond grade school there was a strong oral tradition. They told stories, and it is in the stories they told that they themselves have been preserved. A mile south of our house a pitch stump stands beside the faint trace of an old woodcutter's trail. When I pass by, I think of my father pointing it out to me when I was a child. Right there, he told me, was where my mother's grandfather, Georges Bassette, was found, slumped as if in bloody sleep after his horses drug him to death under a broken load of cordwood. Such was his life that he died for a dollar's worth of pine.

Each winter Margaret and I cut wood to sell the following year. Among the trees are waist-high stumps the woodhawks left, amber-pitched and hard as flint. Old man Bassette and the cordwood cutters have passed beyond living memory, yet in us and the work we continue and the fatwood kindling we take from the stumps, something of him and his kind still lives.

But as we nurtured our own place during the seventies and eighties, the surrounding countryside was subdivided into ranchettes and lots. Hundreds of new houses now surround the three original ranches on our creek, and dozens more will be built this spring. The open space, so necessary for our way of life, has been filled and diminished, and the low, pasturing hills, once muscled with native grass and space, have been wounded beyond all repair by power lines, roads, and fences.

We find ourselves facing an all-too-common American experience, that our good work in creating and caring for our home, while trying to preserve something of a meaningful past, has been overshadowed and threatened by powerful outside forces beyond our control. Our commitment to a custodial relationship with land has been overtaken by speculation and greed, mobility, and money. Our connections to family, neighbors, and community have been strained or severed by conflicts that come with soaring property values and a wildfire market. Our hopes to preserve what we have done here are dulled by a relentless and increasing pressure to cash in and get out.

As for structure, Lisa, what I have in mind is an 80,000 to 90,000-word book made up of relatively short (1,500 to 2,500-word) chapters that follow, in loosely chronological order, specific events in the story of my family, our neighbors, and my own life here, from settlement in the 1880s to the present.

To simplify the task, I'll divide the book into five sections: (1) immigration and settlement, 1880-1950; (2) childhood, 1950-1965; (3) the Vietnam years, 1966-1974; (4) my return to a failing place and its restoration, 1974-1986; and (5) from my parents' deaths in 1987 and 1988 to the present and our continuing efforts here during a time of encroaching urbanization. These sections will likely vary in length. To help me move about in time without making time needlessly complex, I'll begin each section in the present, then loop back to the beginning time of that particular section and move straightforward to its end.

Although I do not have one specific book in mind as a model, the following, among others, will be at my elbow to help guide my way: *A Childhood, the Biography of a Place* by Harry Crews; *Riding the White Horse Home* by Teresa Jordan; *Owning It All* and *Hole in the Sky* by William Kittredge; and *All But the Waltz* by Mary Clearman Blew.

I think *In These Hills* will have an appeal to a variety of readers, including those not closely connected to rural life or the West. It is not, after all, a book about agriculture, but about rediscovering where we belong and ponying up the price of commitment, about tracing connections to those of our people who are gone and the ways we regenerate our pasts, about facing the loss of what we love most while finding hope each day in the work we do. *In These Hills* is about living in America.

I've enclosed two short magazine pieces from a set of four as examples of recent work closely related to subjects I plan to pursue in the book. And I've included two longer essays published in *Harper's* and *Antaeus* that were listed in *Best American Essays*. And for some color, a dust jacket of *The Blind Corral*.

I hope spring comes early after your long hard winter, Lisa, and that the months ahead bring nothing but blue skies.

All the best,

Ralph Beer

COMMENTS

This is a hefty-sized query letter, but the writer is pitching a book, not an article, so the extra room is appropriate. The way this writer writes, though, you quickly forget about its length. He evokes such a mood and paints such clear pictures of the place and the people in it that it's easy to visualize how the book will play out. Beer wrote this synopsis in the form of a letter to his agent, Lisa Bankoff of ICM, upon her advice. "It seemed to work, though," Beer says. "Out of three editors who saw it, we got three offers."

Acquisitions Editor
Hunter Publications

The Florida Where-To-Stay Book

Tens of millions of people visit Florida every year and they all need a place to stay. While most visitors choose hotels, motels, and resorts, others choose condos, private home rentals, bed and breakfasts, country inns, etc. There are accommodations in all price ranges but no guide that covers everything available in every corner of the state. If readers are looking for a beachfront hotel in Pensacola or a country inn in Ocala, this guide lists over four thousand properties to choose from and most have toll-free numbers readers can call for information, literature, special rates, reservations, etc.

The book opens with a chapter on the chain hotels operating in Florida with information on their deals, discounts, general facilities, etc. Addresses are listed for free directories. The bulk of the book is city-by-city alphabetical listings (Alachua, Boyton Beach, Clearwater, Destin, etc.). Each listing is similar to this:

Marina Hotel at St. Johns Place (1515 Prudential Drive, 32207; 904-396-5100, Fax: 904-396-7145, 800-342-4605) 325 rooms and suites, restaurant, lounge, outdoor heated pool, lighted tennis courts, in-room refrigerators, gift shop, a/c, TV, children free with parents, no pets allowed, no-smoking rooms, wheelchair access, airport transportation, 16 meeting rooms, senior rates. SGL/DBL $55-$75.

This could be the first in a series of accommodation guides covering the country. If I've struck a spark of interest, I'll be glad to send you a more detailed outline and sample chapter. Length and format of book is up to the publisher, based on what they think will make the best-selling book. I'm the author of 33 nonfiction books and 1,200 articles on various subjects (computers, travel, lifestyle, reference, etc.).

Sincerely,
Phil Philcox

COMMENTS

This fairly simple, straightforward letter resulted in—are you sitting down?—a 12-book "Where-To-Stay" series of 400- to 500-page guidebooks on different areas of the U.S. Here is Philcox's reasoning on why this particular letter worked: "All of my book sales were the result of a query letter (1-2 pages), followed up with a more detailed outline, sample chapter, etc. I use the same approach for every query: I write as if I were talking to the editor over a cup of coffee—very informal. I explain what the book is in one paragraph or so, why there should be such a book, the audience, and my credits. I feel the short query is enough for them to decide for or against based on the subject and my short presentation. My credits usually convince them I can do the job or at least deserve a more detailed look." I couldn't have said it better.

The Proposal

Those of you unfamiliar with book submissions are probably asking, "What on earth is a proposal? How does it differ from a query? And why are both required?" One way to differentiate between the two is to imagine the query as the rocket that launched the original Mercury astronauts and the proposal is the rocket that sends up the Space Shuttle. In the original Mercury missions, the astronauts basically went straight up and straight down. They were launched by a two-stage booster, they jettisoned their main rocket right after liftoff, and their landing capsule plopped them into the ocean just a few hours later.

Well, that's all a query does. It goes straight out and comes straight back. Its main letter and envelope are ejected shortly after departure, and it returns in an SASE (or hopefully, by way of a call or letter from an interested editor). The mission is deemed either a success ("Great idea. I'd like to assign it to you.") or a failure ("We regret it does not meet our present needs.").

A proposal, on the other hand, is a much more massive undertaking. To launch one of these behemoths, you need two booster rockets (a query *and* a proposal), with the latter propelling you into orbit for weeks before your mission is completed. The proposal is more involved than a magazine query because an agent or an editor needs to see a detailed report and analysis beforehand on what your book will contain, how it will read and look, what its sales projections are, and what your qualifications are to write it.

One final note before I discuss the elements of a proposal. Unless an agent, agency, or publisher specifically says that it welcomes book proposals in lieu of query letters (and I don't know any who do or any reason why they would), do *not* send in your proposal until a query triggers an OK. That said, you shouldn't just sit back, put your feet up on your desk, and wait until your query gets a bite before you get started either. Not only should you have already prepared your proposal by the time you hear back from someone about your query, it's a good idea for you to have finished your proposal before you even *send out* your query. There are two reasons for this.

First, constructing your proposal well before your query will confirm (to yourself) whether you really have a book or not. If you do have enough information to proceed, the proposal process will help you better visualize and fine-tune your concept.

Second, if you get a go-ahead from an agent or publisher from your query, it's paramount that you rush the proposal off immediately while your idea's still fresh and buzzing in the requester's mind. If you wait to start your proposal until you get a "Yes," you can kiss that opportunity goodbye. Proposals are murder to write. Starting from scratch, it could take weeks, maybe longer, for you to research and write it.

That long to write fifteen to twenty pages? Heh-heh-heh. Allow me to introduce you to the five components that comprise a typical nonfiction book proposal, and then you'll understand:

1. Synopsis of the book (one-plus pages).
2. Table of contents (one page).
3. Chapter summaries (ten-plus pages, one to three pages per chapter).
4. Market analysis—cost, demographics, competition, promotion (two-plus pages).
5. Author's qualifications (one page).
   Total length: fifteen-plus pages

Synopsis of the Book (One-Plus Pages)

A proposal doesn't need to grab your reader's attention as suddenly and dramatically as a query does because it's assumed your query has already done that. At this juncture, the agent or editor doesn't want any more sizzle, she wants steak. In this introductory portion of your proposal, your task is to briefly and simply sum up your book's content, theme, tone, structure, main elements, and design suggestions (if any). Since you're not expected to cram everything onto one page, as with a query, you can stretch your legs a bit more here.

Below is the actual synopsis I used to sell this book:

Synopsis

It all begins—or ends—with a query letter. There is no other way into the inner sanctum of magazine and book publishing. If writers want to write for a living, they must learn to master this form of letter writing because every sales pitch they make must follow its precepts. Bottom line: If writers compose poor letters, they will publish few works. This book will show step-by-step how to draft and perfect every type of correspondence writers write: article and book queries, proposals and synopses, cover letters, follow-up letters, rewrite letters, and many other types of written communication.

Other books have been published on how to write query letters, but they've usually painted the topic with a broad brush (how to generate article ideas, how to find markets, how to sell and slant articles). This book will be much more focused, concentrating on the details and mechanics of letter-writing itself. It will explain, for example, the ten specific things editors unconsciously look for in query letters—and the ten bad things. What goes through a writer's mind when he writes a query? What goes through an editor's mind when she reads one? What gratifies a book editor when he goes over a book proposal? What upsets an agent when she scrutinizes a cover letter?

Another unique angle of this book, in addition to instilling and demonstrating letter-writing fundamentals, will be its tone. Each step along the way, readers will be given counsel and tips from two perspectives (twin muses, if you will). One voice will be from the writer's point of view: What are his priorities and expectations regarding writing and selling, what are his needs, concerns, misconceptions regarding editors? The other voice will be from the editor's point of view: What are her priorities and expectations regarding reading and buying, what are her needs, concerns, misconceptions regarding writers? Since the author proposing this book has been a writer, magazine editor and book editor (see "About the Author"), he strongly empathizes with all parties and knows intimately what each one's going through during the crucial and fragile query-writing stage of the writer/editor relationship.

But perhaps the most interesting and helpful aspect of the book will be the unique method by which the various types of letters that writers use are presented and analyzed. Some chapters will feature hypothetical letters corresponding to that chapter's subject (article query, book query, cover letter, etc.). One letter will illustrate an ideal version—the other a mistake-prone version. Various words, phrases, and/or sections of each letter will be highlighted and connected by arrows to explanatory paragraphs in the margins. Each chapter will also feature a short Q&A section relating to issues not covered in the body of the chapter.

Wrapping up some of the chapters will be actual letters that resulted in sales or near-sales to magazines and/or books.

Because this book's subject matter is timeless and its presentation unique, it could become a standard writer's guide for years to come. Readers will not only master the fundamentals of all types of writer's correspondence but, perhaps more important, understand the mind-set of editors, agents, and publishers. With this dual capability at their fingertips, they may discover their future letters may lead to some of their best work—not to mention bylines and checks!

Table of Contents (One Page)

You may get the urge to slough off this portion of your proposal, assuming it's the least-important part. ("Yeh, who reads contents? Has anyone ever bought a book—or not bought one—based on its contents titles?") The temptation, therefore, is to just slap down plain, generic heads for each chapter, figuring the agent or editor doesn't need or want to see catchy titles at this stage, and to turn your attention to the "more important elements" that follow. You're wrong. Never take the table of contents for granted; it's a key factor in any proposal. You should try to come up with the most inspired inscriptions you can think of here.

Let's say you want to write a book on time-management. Which chapter heads would most appeal to a potential buyer—these?

Chapter 1: Time Management
Chapter 2: The Problem of Impatience
Chapter 3: Reorder Your Priorities

Or these?

Chapter 1: How Many People on Their Deathbed
Wish They'd Spent More Time at the Office?
Chapter 2: The Urgency Addiction
Chapter 3: To Live, to Love, to Learn, to Leave a Legacy

The second trio is from best-seller Stephen R. Covey's recent book on time-management, *First Things First*.

Don't overlook design either to perk up your contents page. If you have a computer, your word-processing program is probably equipped with a variety of table of contents templates. Experiment with different formats and fonts and choose one most conducive to the style and tone of your book.

If you intend to write a normal-length book (200-plus pages; 75,000-plus words), try to organize your material into at least eight or nine chapters. If you have fewer chapters than that, you may be packing too much into each one. No reader wants to wade through five novella-size chunks. Plus it looks odd ("Hey, where's the rest of the book?"). Ten short-to-medium ones, however, feel just about right. At the other extreme, too many chapters (more than twenty) look like you're trying to stretch out the book.

Chapter Summaries (Ten-Plus Pages; One to Three Pages Per Chapter)

This section should comprise the bulk (75 percent) of your proposal. The agent or editor expects to see evidence here that you've got meat on the table. A one-paragraph description of each chapter, therefore, won't cut it (unless you're proposing a less-than-average-length book or children's book). One-to-three double-spaced pages is more appropriate and is sufficient to summarize most any passage, touch on all or most of its highlights, and even include a key anecdote, scene, or quote or two. Be careful not to go overboard, though; if your chapter outlines are stretching past three pages, you're liable to start rewriting the whole book, a common trap.

How should your chapter summaries be written? In vivid, conversational style. It should read like an energetic, hard-to-put-down direct-mail advertisement. One of the best examples is Publisher's Clearinghouse. The next time you get one of their mailings, read the copy. I hate to admit it, but the writing in these things is clear, concise, simple, effective—and very persuasive. Their writers won't win any awards, but they get results. Just don't be dull or rattle off reams of data. Although the agent or editor is primarily interested in your content and market potential at this stage—why your book should be published rather than how it will be written—that doesn't mean you can give your zesty wordplay the week off.

Market Analysis (Two-Plus Pages)

This is where it gets beastly. Remember all those days you spent in the catacombs of your college library? Welcome back! This, not the chapter summaries, is the real heavy-lifting portion of your proposal. In this section you must address and allay the nt's or editor's four most crucial concerns:

1. COST—WHAT'S REQUIRED AND HOW MUCH ARE WE TALKING ABOUT?

If you envision your book containing pop-up Walt Disney characters or foldout maps of every major Civil War battlefield, you had better 'fess up now rather than later. Even if your book won't require anything out of the ordinary, devote a paragraph or more to your best ballpark-figure production details:

How many pages will the book run?

How many special elements will it contain (charts, diagrams, photos)?

How long will you need to research and write it?

How much will it cost up front (travel, fees for permissions or artwork)?

2. DEMOGRAPHICS—IS THERE A NEED AND A DESIRE FOR YOUR BOOK?

There had better be a prospective audience out there with plenty of both, and you must show that conclusively. If there isn't, then rethink or revamp your idea until you *do* find a potential readership. Your book must promise something—even if it's pure entertainment. Will they achieve power and success? Learn how to ditch an abusive partner? Find a job? Get to know the real Bill Clinton? Lose weight? Know which computer to buy? Live longer? Confirm how silly cats are?

Find out who reads and buys your type of book and why, how many of these books are published and sold each year, and how many probable customers there are in that group. Throw out these questions to your local librarian and bookstore manager. On their shelves and databases count books similar to yours. Study *Books in Print* and *Forthcoming Books* for other books on your topic. Leaf through periodicals that relate to your book's subject matter for clues as to other likely readers.

If your book is about dog breeding, for example, research how many breeds of dogs there are, how many people own purebred dogs and/or breed them, what kind of people they are (where they live, what they do, how much they earn, etc.), how many attend dog shows, what other books and publications on the topic are out there, etc.

3. COMPETITION—HOW MUCH IS OUT THERE, WHAT DOES IT LACK, AND HOW WILL YOU FILL THE GAP(S)?

You must show why the competition is small, medium, or large and why that is to your advantage. Illustrate how, why, and where your competitors succeed and fail, and how *you* intend to serve that market's readers better. (Bad move: "Gee . . . there really is no competition.") There's *always* competition. The question the agent or editor wants you to answer is, What's different or better about your book that will slam-dunk your rivals? For example, store shelves currently groan from the weight of all the motivational-success books that have been published recently. To convince an agent or an editor to take on *your* motivational-success book, show how clearly and substantially different your premise is from the others. Does yours have a unique slant? Will you organize and present the material better? Are you going to add new and/or different topics? Are your graphics going to be more user-friendly and/or creative? Are you promising more pages?

4. PROMOTION—WHO OR WHAT CAN HELP SELL YOUR BOOK?

"Uh, excuse me, isn't that the publisher's role? I'm just a writer, not P.T. Barnum." Technically, yes, promotion is the publisher's bailiwick. But let me, if I may, answer for the publisher here: Are you Robert Fulghum? Carolyn See? Colin Powell? The Pope? If you are, then you may skip this section (in fact, you don't even need this book) because the publisher will spend 163% of its budget promoting your book so it can be assured of selling enough copies to pay back the gazillion-dollar advance you squeezed out of it and the mega-copy print run it committed itself to.

If you aren't one of publishing's elite, then the promotional budget for your opus will probably total in the amount of, oh gosh, how much loose change do you have on you? Seriously, though, no matter how much it is, it will never be enough. Therefore, whatever *you* can do to help promote your book will go a long way toward convincing a potentially lukewarm agent or editor that your book suddenly makes good sense.

To do that, you must overwhelm the agent or editor with all the potential markets out there for it. For example, if your book is about home-office computing, point out all the myriad ways and places it could be sold or advertised:

Computer stores
Computer books, magazines, and newsletters

Computer shows

Computer classes

Computer clubs

On-line services

Office-furniture stores

Department stores

Small-business associations and/or clubs

Small-business books, magazines, and newsletters

Home-business books, magazines, and newsletters

Home-business associations and/or clubs

In addition to showing where your book could be sold, show how your book can be promoted, either by yourself or others. What experts, celebrities, or famous friends do you know who could plug it with cover endorsements or reviews? Have you ever appeared on TV or radio—you might make a good talk-show guest and promote your book there. Do you ever speak at conferences—what a marvelous opportunity to plop down a few dozen copies of your book right by the exit. Do you publish a newsletter or write a column—just think of the shameless publicity you could foist on your captive audience.

Author's Qualifications (One Page)

Because much more money, time, and effort rest on the sale of a book than on the sale of a magazine or newspaper article, your experience, expertise, reputation—in short, your credentials—may be more crucial in some cases than even your content to the decisionmakers who will ultimately have to decide whether to publish it or not.

Therefore, be as detailed and specific as you can when writing this part of your proposal. Why are you the most qualified to write this book? Why should an agent or an editor not even consider anyone else? Inundate the reader with so much relevant background and connections you have to your subject matter that, rather than worrying about minor questions she may have about your book, all she'll be able to think about is what dire consequences could result if she turned you down and such a lapse was discovered later! If you sell the reader on *you*, any qualms she may have about your book will lessen considerably. As in a magazine query, don't mention *everything* you've done. Listing your background doesn't mean laying out your entire resume. Mention every experience that's relevant to your project—but not one item more.

That's a brief overview of how to write a nonfiction book proposal. The five general requirements I've outlined are basically the same for most proposals, but each agent or editor will have her own particular preferences and policies (see "Questions & Answers" for more detail on how proposal requirements can often differ greatly depending on who you send it to).

To give you an idea of what an actual, full-length nonfiction book proposal looks like, I asked author and freelance writer Susan Goodman to help me out. Beginning on the next page is the actual book proposal she used to pitch her recent children's book, *Scouts' Honor: The Great Antler Auction*. It's shorter than a normal proposal would be because it's for a children's book, but all five required elements are in place.

Ideal Nonfiction Book Proposal

OVERVIEW

We are all constantly bombarded by media stories of dwindling wildlife and species extinction. Children seem to be the group that feels these losses most passionately. At the same time, they are the ones most powerless to counteract the problem. But not always, not everywhere. About 125 kids in Jackson Hole, Wyoming, are helping the last great migrating elk herd in the United States not only to come back from near extinction, but to survive and flourish.

Local Boy Scouts are the only people authorized to collect the elk antlers shed each spring on the National Elk Refuge outside of Jackson Hole. The third Saturday each May, the scouts auction these antlers to the artists, mountain men, tourists, and international business people who gather to bid on these valuable, sought-after horns. In 1993, for example, the auction brought in $75,078 and somewhere between 80 and 90 percent of it will help keep the elk from starving this winter.

The annual Elk Antler Auction is one of the rare win/win situations in conservation: Buyers are pleased with their purchases; the Boy Scouts pull off a splendidly good deed; the very animals who grew these precious antlers are fed from the revenues of their sale. Surprisingly, this event has never been written about in anything more far-reaching than a newspaper. Yet, it is a tale anyone could love, especially children, who can proudly identify with their counterparts in Jackson who are helping the elk survive.

Scout's Honor, a nonfiction book for middle readers, will capture the drama and excitement of this success story for its young audience. Its full-color photographs and text will follow the Jackson Hole scouts as they hunt for antlers in the National Elk Refuge against the grandeur of the Grand Teton Mountains. *Scout's Honor* will record the scouts' realizations and reactions as they learn about the elk and prepare for the sale. By the time the auctioneer brings his gavel down for the last time, our readers will understand exactly what the scouts' accomplishments mean for the elk, wildlife conservation, and their own personal growth.

Where *Scout's Honor* will clearly revolve around the scouts and their efforts, the second story woven through the book is the history of the elk herd, its near decimation and gradual recovery. As Jackson Hole novelist, Donald Hough, wrote in *Snow Above Town*: "The elk herd is the greatest single thing about the valley, and to a very real extent so is its fate."

In a recent report on its four-year study, "Benchmarks in Science Literacy," a commission appointed by the American Academy for the Advancement of Science has urged sweeping reforms for the nation's science curricula. Among other things, the commission has recommended teaching science in ways that connect it to the arts, humanities, and vocational subjects. *Scout's Honor* is a perfect book for such contextual learning. It starts with nature and the ecology of the elk herd, then explores its reach into the history of western settlement, medicine, economics, and the fine arts.

Furthermore, *Scout's Honor* will appeal to educators looking for more sophisticated approaches to conservation than "Save the Whale" slogans and more integrated solutions to environmental issues than entreaties to recycle. Feeding its lessons through the drama of children's experiences, *Scout's Honor* will also be an engaging choice for teachers committed to using nonfiction trade books to teach the whole-language method of reading.

Since schools all over the country are increasing their commitment to science and conservation issues, we propose marketing *Scout's Honor* directly to groups like the National Science Teachers Association and publications like *Book Links*. Yet there is another important market for *Scout's Honor*. Other scouts and scout leaders will doubtless be interested in these events at Jackson Hole. There are 4,625,800 Boy Scouts in the United States alone, another 1,170,000 in Britain and the Commonwealth countries.

Scout's Honor will be the second collaboration between author Susan Goodman and photographer Michael Doolittle. This book will draw upon many of the strengths established by this team in their first effort, *Bats, Bugs, and Biodiversity: Adventures in the Amazonian Rain Forest*, which chronicles a week when a group of American school children visit the Peruvian jungle. Both books combine a strong narrative line with nature and science; they portray kids, animals, and unbelievable scenery in lush photographs.

Goodman has done extensive writing for children including a video on wetlands for the Library Science Center near Ellis Island, work for The National Geographic Society's Educational Division, and another nonfiction science book for middle readers, *Unseen Rainbows, Silent Songs: The World Beyond Our Senses*. As a contributing editor for the General Learning Corporation, a company that creates curriculum materials, she has spent over a decade writing about scientific and sociological issues at junior and senior high school levels.

Photographer Michael Doolittle has had his pictures published in a variety of books and magazines including *The Rainforests* (Smithmark Press), *Discovering Rainforests* (Publications International), *National Geographic Traveler*, and the Cousteau Society's *Dolphin Log*. He covered the first children's workshop for *National Geographic World*. He has been a naturalist/guide at the Tambopata Nature Reserve in Peru.

FORMAT

We envision *Scout's Honor* as a forty-page book, complete with a table of contents, chapters, glossary, index, and a list of further suggested reading. Most of the full-color photographs will directly illustrate the text, but others will use detailed captions as an opportunity to provide additional information. Chapter two will also use historical pictures as illustration.

Some artwork will be required: a map and an occasional line drawing to illustrate a sidebar.

CONTENT

The narrative of *Scout's Honor* will follow the Jackson Hole troupe as they comb the refuge for antlers, sort and package them, and participate in the auction. Although it will draw upon the experience of the entire group, *Scout's Honor* will focus upon a few specific scouts—their ties to nature, their feelings about the elk, their pride in their own accomplishments. The story will include snippets of actual conversation and (if we can induce the kids to write them) entries from their journals about these experiences. Although a good deal of science and natural history will be woven into the main text, we are committed to a dramatic narrative that focuses upon the scouts and their adventure. As noted below, subjects like migration patterns, the region's natural history, uses of elk horn, and the complex issues of wildlife conservation will be put into sidebars positioned as a natural outgrowth of the scouts' story.

CHAPTER 1: Our story will begin with the thump of the auctioneer's gavel at the 27th annual Elk Antler Auction. This brief chapter will quickly provide background information and introduce us to some of the book's central characters. It will also weave in questions, feelings, and issues to be resolved in subsequent chapters.

CHAPTER 2: This chapter will tell the history of elk in the high country around Jackson Hole. It will explain how human settlement cut off migration routes and food sources until so many elk died around the turn of the century that one settler said, "You could step on the carcasses of elk and walk for a mile without ever stepping off." The National Elk Refuge began in 1912 and has turned a good quarter of their original winter pasture back to the elk. This acreage is still not sufficient for the elk to survive on without supplemental feeding and that's where our scouts come in.

The sidebar in this chapter will look at the other wildlife living in the Refuge: moose, bison, bighorn sheep, coyotes, trumpeter swans, osprey, and bald eagles.

CHAPTER 3: On the third Saturday in April, the scouts set out to gather the four tons of antlers that male elk annually shed on the Refuge before moving into the Tetons and South Yellowstone for spring. This chapter is a good opportunity for humor as the scouts scramble through brush and over the Refuge's twenty-five thousand acres hunting for horns. They may well flush out some competition, for animals like porcupine and squirrel value the calcium that comes from nibbling on an antler. The chapter's sidebar will use the elks' migration as a jumping-off point to describe more about the elk themselves, their life cycle, and a typical year's activities.

CHAPTER 4: In the week before the auction, the scouts meet in a secret location because elk antlers have become so valuable they must be hidden from possible theft. The scouts and their leaders work each evening to sort, bundle, tape, and weigh the antlers. They group antlers of different hues and sizes together to appeal to different buyers. Some artists, for example, make inlaid belt buckles out of the nubby antler butts, where others prefer vaulting horns to create chairs, tables, or chandeliers. The sidebar will discuss horn and why it's so desirable, then show some of the products made from antlers, everything from cribbage boards and knife handles to remedies in Eastern medicine that make powdered elk horn a multimillion dollar business in Asia.

CHAPTER 5: Jackson Hole's four mammoth elk-antler arches serve as a dramatic backdrop to the bundles of horns set out on auction day. Scouts lug horns taller than themselves up to be bid upon by actors, artists, and agents for Asian businesses, people who are willing to pay up to twenty-five dollars a pound for elk antlers. This chapter will be a fine climax to the story, filled with the color of the audience, the excitement of the scouts, and the drama of the auction as prices and earnings mount ever higher. By the end of the auction, the scouts will have raised many thousands of dollars to help the elk get through another winter. This accomplishment is a natural lead-in to a sidebar on the recovery of the elk herd.

CHAPTER 6: The denouement, this chapter will picture the Refuge in winter. In its opening vignette, a scout will accompany the refuge manager through the thick snow to feed the elk some of the thirty tons of alfalfa they will require over the winter. Thoughts and feelings of our profiled scouts will show the readers what they have gained by their experience. This chapter's last look at the elk will show the readers what we all have gained by the herd's conservation. The sidebar will tackle the complexity of conservation.

BACKGROUND INFORMATION

The Elk Antler Auction has been held each year since 1968. The Boy Scouts gather the antlers on the Refuge during the third weekend in April. Then, after grouping the horns for sale a few days before, the scouts auction them off on the third Saturday in May. The activities are so well organized that it will be easy for us to go in on three separate occasions and take part. Furthermore, it is so well-established that these auctions—and, consequently, *Scout's Honor*'s freshness as a book reporting on an event—will continue through the years.

We have already discussed our project with Vic Lindeburg, head of the auction for the Jackson Hole Boy Scouts, and Jim Griffin, manager of the National Elk Refuge. Both have given the project their hearty endorsement and promise their full cooperation. Griffin has offered to let us ride out with them to feed the elk and guide us to the moose, bighorn sheep, bison, etc., in the Refuge.

COMMENTS

Goodman covers a lot of ground in these few pages. You can really visualize how the book will look from her vivid—yet concise—description, especially in her chapter summaries. It's clear she has thought this project out completely and that there's definitely a book here. My only qualm: I would have preferred to see jazzier chapter titles written in kid lingo, but who am I to quibble with success? *Scouts' Honor: The Great Antler Auction* was published by Simon & Schuster.

Questions & Answers

Q: It's hard enough fitting an article query onto one page. But how do I describe a three hundred-page book in a single sheet?

A: Since you can't get your hands on actual successful nonfiction book queries, other than those in this book, do the next best thing: Study what most resembles them. Go to your local bookstore or library. Pick up a half dozen nonfiction books similar to your idea and read the jacket and back-cover copy. Do the same thing at your video store. Stroll through the nonfiction sections (documentaries, hobbies, how-to's, sports, fitness, etc.) and read the promo copy on the back of the boxes. In both cases you'll see the contents of an entire book or program summarized quite effectively in just a snippet of copy. None of these sketches will contain more words than a standard one-page letter—but they'll sure hook you into buying or renting them, won't they?

The reason they work is because they play up the story's or program's highlights—and dispense with the rest. They use key words and phrases, fast pacing, and a formulaic structure to push the hot buttons that most appeal to us. Read enough of them and you'll eventually start to see the consistent factors that make them work. Then instill those in your book queries.

Q: You say I can query an agent or an editor on a nonfiction book concept without having written one word of my book beforehand. Well, if I haven't started it yet, how can I possibly describe it?

A: If you don't even have a rough idea of what your book is about, then clearly you're not ready to send a query letter yet. A good rule of thumb is, don't send a query until you're able to send a proposal. Your book should be pretty well laid out by the query stage, chapter by chapter, and you should have researched who will buy it, how many similar books exist, how yours differs, and different ways to market it.

Q: Writers aren't supposed to seek an editor's input before writing a query, but I can't conceive of starting a book proposal without some prior editorial guidance. Aren't some proposals prepared in tandem with an agent or editor?

A: Yes, occasionally. If your book query sparks interest, the agent or editor you sent it to will contact you by phone or letter and ask for a detailed proposal. Some individuals will leave it at that and simply wait for your proposal. Others will go farther: "We'd like to see a proposal, and here's what we want in it . . ." If you're fortunate to get someone like this, you'll progress into discussions on how to prepare and customize the proposal to their needs. For example, if your reader is an agent, she'll probably have a few editors in mind at several publishing houses she's considering sending the proposal to and will give you insight on what style, content, and structure they prefer. She may tell you that the editor at Publisher A rates qualifications higher than the one at Publisher B, or that the editor at Publisher C prefers to see just chapter summaries and no table of contents, or that the editor at Publisher D likes her market analyses filled out on her company's own special sheet, or whatever. If your reader is an editor, she'll have even more precise information about what her editorial board favors—and what it hates.

In these cases you may have to run your proposal through a couple of drafts (like I did with this book) before your agent or editor gives the OK to formally present it, but when it's finally ready, it will stand a much better chance of passing muster than if you hadn't gotten this special care and attention. Can't hope for anything better than that!

CHAPTER SIX

The Novel Query and Synopsis

". . . But enough about me. Let's talk about my novel."
Arthur Masear cartoon

I don't think I'm going too far out on a limb by saying the dream of most writers is to pen a novel. It is the ultimate test of one's creativity, writing acumen, dedication, patience, and masochistic limits. It is the Big Book, the great American you-know-what. No matter how successful you may become or have already become in your writing career, until you have written and published a novel, you will never be able to adequately answer the most unceasingly asked question you will get during your lifetime: "So, when are you gonna to write a *real* book?"

It's an unfair question, of course. We're fortunate if *anything* we write is published, let alone a book, and certainly a novel. For those of you out there who feel or felt compelled to write one, however, and who dream of becoming the next Michael Crichton or Danielle Steel, this chapter will show you how to deliver your package into the right hands and how to convince the agents and editors who receive it that *your* story is the "must read" they've been waiting for.

I'm presuming, of course, that your book has already been written. If it hasn't, then stop right here—you'll save us all a lot of time and effort. You see, a novel isn't like a nonfiction book, which can get a go-ahead from a publisher before you've written word one. These delicate works of art must be judged on their final draft only. Fiction either works or it doesn't; you can't tinker with it afterwards like you can with nonfiction. And you can't assign it like a common article or a nonfiction book; it's too quirky and subjective. Although a novel requires no detailed market analysis up front and your background and expertise mean zip, you've got to write the whole enchilada beforehand—and knock the reader's socks off on their first read. For these reasons, an agent or an editor would be daft to offer a contract for a half-finished or a sight-unseen novel. Therefore, for everyone's sake, finish the monster first.

Does that mean, though, that once you've typed those magic words, "The End," on the last page of your novel, you're ready to rent that limo and start "taking lunch" with agents or publishers? No. And here's why. The tendency of many first novelists, after they've finished the final polish of the final draft of the final chapter and are basking in the headiness of their achievement, is to delude themselves into thinking it's ready to submit. "Sure, it's still got some problems—the third and fourth chapters slow down the pace I set in the first two, I never did figure out my sidekick's motivation for stealing the gold, and my dialogue in places isn't as witty as the rest— but hell, it's *done* and I'm *tired*. If I want to send it out to see if it might impress somebody, I deserve that. I'll worry about perfecting it later."

Wrong. You only have one shot at each agency or publisher, so don't squander these valuable opportunities with submissions that are less than perfect or complete. Agents and editors are not in the novel-development business, they are in the novel-selling and -buying business. And they can't sell or buy anything that's still a work-in-progress—even if 95 percent of the work has progressed. New York agent Donald Maass of Donald Maass Literary spoke at the Greater Dallas Writers' Association's 12th Craft of Writing Conference in 1994 and said that one of the most common mistakes authors make is to send out manuscripts they aren't 100 percent satisfied with. They've done all they wanted to do, Maass said. But that's not good enough. The competition is so stiff and overwhelming out there, he said, that unless you know in your heart that your book is exactly the way you want it, is absolutely the best work you have ever done and could ever do, that you have no doubts or qualms about any aspect of it, then do not send it out because it will come back.

Once your book *is* done and ready, however, you're still only three-fourths of the way there. You then need a dynamite teaser campaign to sell it. And that's what this chapter will show you how to do. The sales tool I recommend is an all-in-one submission arranged in two parts: a Query and a Synopsis, both sent in at the same time. If the reader is attracted by this twin-salvo pitch, she'll next ask to see either some actual finished chapters or, if she's really excited, your entire book.

Why do you need both a query and a synopsis, and what's the difference? The best way to describe what each of these elements does and why they're important is to visualize your book as an upcoming movie. Your query is the movie's poster, your synopsis is the movie's coming attractions. Ideally, you want both to hit the viewer simultaneously to pique her interest so much that she'll run right out and see the movie.

Your "poster's" job is like the proverbial 2 × 4's—to get her attention. If your poster boasts a great title, a juicy plot, intriguing characters, a fascinating setting, and a teaser line that lures her in, it will leave her panting for more. "This sounds great! I can't wait for the coming attractions. When will they be out?"

Look no farther, just turn the page. Your synopsis will then follow up with a fast-paced, chapter-by-chapter summary of the entire book, revealing the plot and subplots, all major characters, key scenes and dialogue—even the ending. If both parts of your presentation come off as they should, your reader may even buy a ticket to your extravaganza. Here's how to make her do that.

The Query

If you hate queries (and who doesn't), then you'll be happy to know that novel queries don't resemble article or nonfiction book queries much at all. Most of the other Commandments discussed in this book are unnecessary for novel queries.

So what *is* required? I'll answer that question simply: "What's your book about?" That's it. Simply write down what you tell people when they ask that question. If you, like me, never tire of hearing that question, you'll relish the opportunity to talk up your book's plot and characters. It's like someone asking about your first child—who wouldn't want to brag a little? OK—a lot!

The problem with some writers' queries, however, is that they get carried away with doing just that—they describe too much of themselves and/or their book. Agent Maass says novice novelists are so anxious to impress an agent in their letter that they're afraid to leave *anything* out. "You get these single-spaced letters that fill the entire page—from the very top to the very bottom, from the extreme left-hand edge to the extreme right-hand edge. They know they're supposed to keep it to one page, but they're afraid you're not going to notice or care about them or their book unless they tell you everything. They're more eager to have me affirm who they are than to simply tell their story."

All writers fall into this trap. A few years ago when I was churning out my first try at a novel, whenever a conversation turned to writing (and even many times when it didn't) I found myself steering the topic to me and my book—just so I could launch into another description of it. I'm sure I turned off a lot of friends and acquaintances, I felt ashamed for my boorishness, and it showed an utter lack of tact . . . but I kept doing it anyway. Hey, it was my novel!

Well, now's *your* chance; just make sure you do it the right way. Unlike article and nonfiction book queries, which have ten commandments, novel queries have only six firm requisites. Each query letter must, in order:

1. TARGET 'EM AT THE TOP

As with all other queries, make sure you send your letter to the right agent or editor (i.e., someone who has recently handled a similar book). Many agents and editors specialize in certain genres (mysteries, romance, horror, etc.). It stands to reason, therefore, that if your book is a western, your chances will be better if, instead of sending your query arbitrarily to the William Morris Agency or Simon & Schuster, you send it to an agent or an editor who can't get enough of westerns; who lives, eats, and sleeps westerns.

The previous chapter explained how to identify and track down agents of authors who have written books similar to yours. Follow those same steps here. This will assure you that your submission will be read by one of the most receptive readers you could possibly hope for.

2. GRAB 'EM FROM THE START

Somewhere up front—centered across your page, in your lead, or in your first paragraph—slap down your book's title. Under that title place a short description or subtitle (similar to the "deck" that magazines run under their article titles):

> "An unspeakable crime
> A town ripped apart
> As the nation awaits a verdict . . ."
> *(From John Grisham's* A Time to Kill*)*

"Under a new president,
the future of the Air Force—and the nation—
hangs in the balance . . .
    (*From Dale Brown's* Chains of Command*)*

"He was their son,
their pride and joy—
then the unthinkable occurred . . .
    (*From Danielle Steel's* Vanished*)*

Another effective way is to create a one-sentence-says-it-all summation of your book, called the "hook" or "handle":

"Thelma and Louise meet Beavis and Butt-head"
"A cross between *The Firm* and *The Manchurian Candidate*"
"The Predator gets lost in Jurassic Park"

3. WOW 'EM IN THE MIDDLE

Paint the most appealing, absorbing, and mouth-watering description you can of the book's main characters, plot, and subplots. Don't just state the genre to your readers, immerse them in it. Don't just describe the atmosphere, airlift them into it. Good examples, for both length and style, are hardcover book jackets, paperback back-covers, and publisher's catalogs.

One exemplary model is this hardcover flap copy from Frederick Forsyth's *The Fist of God*. If you were an agent or an editor, wouldn't *you* want to see more?

From the behind-the-scenes decision-making of the Allies to the secret meetings of Saddam Hussein's war cabinet, from the brave American fliers running their dangerous missions over Iraq to the heroic young spy planted deep in the heart of Baghdad.

Unless the Allies can penetrate the Iraqi regime, they fear they will be sending the vast coalition of air and land forces they have mobilized after the invasion of Kuwait into a bloody desert Armageddon. Then word leaks out to British intelligence that Israel's Mossad had once run a mole in Iraq itself—someone in the highest levels of Saddam's government whose identity even the Mossad had never been able to discover. This is the mysterious "Jericho," and into Baghdad, under the very eyes of Iraq's fearsome secret police, goes Major Mike Martin of Britain's elite Special Air Service Regiment, disguised as an Arab and determined to reestablish the connection with Jericho.

It is a most dangerous game. Moreover, while Jericho can convey—for a price—inside information about what is going on in the high councils of the Iraqi dictator, Saddam has kept his ultimate weapon secret even from his most trusted advisers. The nightmare scenario that haunts General Schwarzkopf and his colleagues is suddenly imminent unless, somehow, Mike Martin can locate that weapon in time.

Peopled with vivid characters, brilliantly displaying the intricacies of intelligence operations, both electronic and human, moving back and forth between Washington and London, Baghdad and Kuwait, desert vastnesses and city bazaars, *The Fist of God* is a breathtaking novel that tells the utterly convincing story of what may actually have happened behind the headlines.

4. IMPRESS 'EM ON THE TURN

If you know of any marketing or promotional tie-in to your book or subject matter, mention it briefly: "With everyone talking about alien abductions right now—two nonfiction books on the bestseller list, tabloids unearthing abductees every other week, Oprah admitting she was yanked, Stephen Spielberg's next movie, and the recent Congressional investigation—the time may be right for my novel, *I Was a Martian Hostage*."

5. REASSURE 'EM AT THE END

Good news! Your qualifications are not as important to a novel's success as they are to a nonfiction book's so you can breathe easy—you don't have to be a spy to sell that spy novel or a Fabio fan to pen romance novels. All that counts in a novel, thank goodness, is how well you tell a story. You may be the world's foremost bowhunter, but that skill won't help you weave a taut, pulse-pounding plot for your wilderness thriller; create unforgettable heroes, heroines, and villains; and describe a snow-packed forest setting that sends chills down the reader's back. Your expertise with a bow-and-arrow *will* help you, however, if you're writing a how-to nonfiction book on bowhunting.

Nevertheless, although expertise, background, and even previous writing experience won't help much in selling your detective novel, it won't *hurt* to mention if you've written books, published articles, or ever been a detective. Just keep it brief.

6. INDUCE 'EM TO ACT

Tired of waiting two or three months to hear back from an agent or a publisher? Then make it easy on yourself *and* those poor souls to whom you're sending your queries. Instead of an SASE, enclose a stamped, self-addressed *postcard* and type on the back:

_____ Please send sample chapters

_____ Please send complete manuscript

_____ Idea doesn't interest us at this time

As a writer, I not only get more responses back this way but I get them back much quicker. As an editor, I can send them back the same day I get them—either I buy them, I reject them, or I scribble down their status if I can't give an immediate answer ("Still considering it—it's with the editor-in-chief now"). In any case, you aren't kept waiting interminably.

Total length of novel query letter: one to two pages

To illustrate how these six novel-query requisites would look together in one letter, I created a hypothetical Ideal Novel Query Letter on the next page.

Ideal Novel Query Letter

1.

> James Smith
> Smith & Jones Literary Agency
> 123 Fifth Avenue
> New York, NY 10000
> Dear Mr. Smith:

2.

> ## Red Blood Rising
> *What if Indians went on the warpath again?*

3.

> What if, in 1996, an Indian leader named John Proud emerges—the savior his people have been waiting for—who combines the charisma of John F. Kennedy, the oratory of Jesse Jackson, and the worldwide appeal of Gandhi? The Martin Luther King of Indians.
>
> What if a second, even more powerful, Indian figure named Tomatoken also arises, a direct descendant of Cochise, who preaches confrontation and secession from the U.S.? The Malcolm X of Indians.
>
> What if, overnight, the two make the dormant Indian movement bigger than the antiwar movement, more popular than the women's movement, and more violent than the civil-rights movement?
>
> What if a beautiful Los Angeles anchorwoman, Leslie Brandt, uncovers a diabolical plot—by a secret group of government extremists—to infiltrate the Grand Canyon, commit a series of shocking Indian-style atrocities, and pin them on the Indians, thus effectively destroying the Indian movement?

1. TARGET 'EM AT THE TOP

This writer sent his query to this particular agent for a reason—the agent recently handled a thriller similar to this writer's book. Short of actually working in an agency and knowing who everybody is, what they specialize in, and what they personally like to see, sending your query to someone who has recently handled a similar book is the best method yet devised to avoid the slush-pile.

2. GRAB 'EM FROM THE START

The first thing a browser sees on a bookstore shelf is the title, so come up with a good one and slap it down up front and center. This writer bettered that by also adding a "hook" underneath it.

3. WOW 'EM IN THE MIDDLE

This book is a thriller, so the writer penned his plot in traditional thriller book-jacket style. Try to match the style of your letter to the genre of your book.

3.

What if Billy Hyde, a young boy on family vacation, survives the first grisly attack and becomes the only person alive who knows the identity of the killers—a three-man team of international assassins led by the cruel and efficient Austrian, Hans Metel?

And what if everyone heads for the Grand Canyon in a final, desperate race to find Billy first, who is close to death himself and who must use all his wiles to not only survive the grueling desert conditions, but outwit his ruthless pursuers and foil one of the most fiendish conspiracies in modern times?

From the Hopi Snake Ceremony in Arizona to a skinhead pub in England, from a hellish blizzard high atop Mount McKinley to deep within a Louisiana swamp. Indian ghosts, secret caves, cop killings, helicopter rescues, medicine men, soccer goons, vision quests, and a particularly malevolent nest of rattlesnakes are the chief elements of *Red Blood Rising*.

4.

The subject of Indians has probably never been more popular. Spawned, in part, by a renewed interest in America's cultural diversity and heritage; by best-sellers with Indian themes such as Tony Hillerman's novels; by movies such as *Dances With Wolves*, *Thunderheart*, *Last of the Mohicans*, *Geronimo*, and *Pocahontas*; by documentaries such as *Incident at Oglala* and Ted Turner's mammoth thirty million-dollar miniseries, it is clear that a novel about Indians set in the present day would be a natural—especially if, as in this case, the Indians aren't all portrayed as the "bad guys."

4. IMPRESS 'EM ON THE TURN

It never hurts to throw in a few statistics, some research, and promotional angles if you can think of any. Even the most erudite agent or editor isn't up on *everything*. This writer obviously did his homework. Such data could persuade a hesitant agent to say, "Hmm, I never knew about that. Maybe I *should* look at this."

1.

I decided to contact you because of your expertise with similar thrillers such as John Brown's *Indian Moon* for Tripleday. Enclosed is a synopsis of the book. I've completed the entire manuscript.

5. REASSURE 'EM AT THE END

If your background and qualifications are relevant to your book, say so. This writer included everything that mattered, and more important, left out everything that didn't.

5.

As for my qualifications, I've been an editor for ten years at *Indian Times*, the largest Indian newspaper in the country (more than one hundred fifty thousand readers). In 1992 I helped edit and cowrite a special series of articles on Indian casinos that was nominated for a National Magazine Award. From 1989 to 1991 I served as an editorial consultant for the Bureau of Indian Affairs. I've lectured to various cultural and writer's organizations and annually judge the Fort Apache Short Story Contest. As for my writing, I've published articles in *Esquire*, *Newsday*, and many other publications.

6. INDUCE 'EM TO ACT

A simple P.S. is all it takes to save stamps *and* speed up an agent's or an editor's reply.

6.

Sincerely,

Frank Williams
555 Madison Way
Anytown, WI 22222
414-555-1212
414-5551213 (fax)

P.S. Please note on the enclosed postcard if you would like to see sample chapters or the complete manuscript. No need to return the synopsis. Thank you.

Sample Letters

Dear Russell Galen,

I am a contributing editor (and the former senior editor) at *Men's Health*, a national magazine with a press run of one million. I've just completed my first novel, *Ember From the Sun*, the story of a Neanderthal girl born and raised in the 1990s.

A year ago, I read a *Time* magazine article about the five-thousand-year-old "Iceman" of the Austrian Alps; it began with the line, **"Women have inquired about the possibility of having his baby."** Bingo—the premise of my story hit me: "What if scientists discovered an intact Neanderthal who was pregnant with a still-viable embryo?" The cover blurb for my novel could read:

> *Paleoanthropologist Hans Heimler uncovers the scientific treasure of the millenia: a 45,000-year-old Neanderthal preserved in arctic ice, and in her womb, a tiny, frozen embryo. He implants the embryo in a surrogate mother, and Ember, a Neanderthal girl, is born in 1990. The baby is adopted and raised among the Quanoot Indians of Whaler Bay, Washington. As Ember struggles to understand why she is different and to know the purpose of her extraordinary gifts, her quest is driven by visions of a band of mysterious, golden-skinned people, the last survivors of their race, who are fleeing genocide. Somehow, their rescue depends on her. But as she unravels the veil that hides her answers, Heimler returns, with his own claims on her life.*

I hold a journalism degree from the University of Florida, and began my writing career in 1980 as a newspaper feature writer. My features have appeared in the *Miami Herald, St. Petersburg Times, Baltimore Sun, Denver Post, San Francisco Chronicle*, and in other newspapers and magazines. *USA Today* and other newspapers and radio talk shows have commented on my articles in *Men's Health*; recent pieces include a profile of a Cherokee man who is the army's top wilderness survival instructor and a look at the biological roots of war. My short fiction has appeared in *Aboriginal Science Fiction* magazine, and my poem, "For Ecstatic Dance," was performed in several productions by the Still Moving Dance Company.

Judging from the stream of books and articles on the subject, readers remain as fascinated by prehistoric peoples as they were when the *Clan of the Cave Bear* series clung to the top of the bestseller lists.

I researched Neanderthals and early humans for two months before I sat down to write

Ember From the Sun. I've enclosed the first chapter. Would you like to see the rest of the manuscript? I've queried four other literary agents at the same time.

Thank you,

Mark Canter

P.S. I enjoyed reading your columns in *Writer's Digest*.

COMMENTS

I'll let New York agent Russell Galen of Scovil, Chichak, Galen Literary Agency do the honors here. He was so impressed with this novel query that he devoted his entire "New York Overheard" column to it in *Writer's Digest* (September 1994): "Once I read his letter, I knew this was a manuscript I had to see. First, I made sure the other agents didn't stand a chance: I called Canter that minute to have him rush the manuscript to me, and read it the instant it came in.

"I get five to ten letters a day similar to Canter's. What was there about his that made me drop what I was doing and call him? First, it was a good-looking, laser-printed letter, of the right length (about 300 words). It had the mark of professionalism. Second, Canter seemed to understand that while he had a page of stuff to say, what I really wanted was the *hook*. He carefully crafted a 60-word summary and set it off from the rest of the letter by indenting the left and right margins an extra half-inch to draw the eye. Third, the hook was a winner.

"Man, you should have seen what happened. Fifteen copies of *Ember*'s manuscript went to fifteen editors on a Monday, and by Thursday all hell broke loose. The minute editors heard about this book, they had to read it—and even at 800 pages people were finishing it on the second or third day. Not only were the editors talking to me, they were talking to their friends. (This is the Great High Holy Miracle of agentry known as *buzz*.) Dozens of calls came in from people who had heard about the book through the buzz: foreign publishers, movie producers, audio publishers. On Thursday the book was auctioned to Delacorte Press for $250,000, a stupendous advance for a first novel by an unknown new writer. It is tentatively scheduled for publication in Spring 1996."

Dear David Hale Smith,

John is currently out of the city, but I relayed your message to him. He has already obtained new representation but thanks you for your interest.

Perhaps your communication will not be entirely wasted, however. Coincidentally, I am seeking some specialized representation for a recently completed book of my own.

Briefly, I am a published genre novelist with an ongoing multi-book deal at a major New York house (HarperCollins) who is releasing my books at the rate of one per year. With completed titles in the pipeline through 1997, I became a little bored with horror and turned my attention to a longtime pet project based on years as a world-traveling network TV documentarian.

The Poison Tree is a gut-wrenching, street-level exposition of political terror as it affects the children who grow up radicalized by political and religious hatreds. The book follows one teenaged terrorist from the bloody streets of Belfast to the moneyed boulevards of Beverly Hills in a dangerous plot that can only end in death.

David, I am specifically seeking an agent with both the time and the connections to "power-rep" *The Poison Tree* on a high-level auction basis for print and film. As a screenwriter (with a major film deal for my first book) and hot novelist (Harper's six-figure, multi-book buy was unprecedented for a first-timer) I am convinced *The Poison Tree* will be a best-selling political thriller.

If this concept interests you, and you would like to discuss *The Poison Tree*, I would be pleased to hear from you.

Sincerely,

Michael O'Rourke

COMMENTS

This shows how even experienced writers still have to hustle to sell their work, what can be accomplished if they're resourceful, and what role serendipity can sometimes play. In this particular case, another writer, an unpublished novelist, sent an introductory letter to Dallas agent Smith on his friend O'Rourke's fax machine. Smith sent back an encouraging letter thanking him and briefly describing his agency and the kind of material he preferred to see. The writer was out of town when Smith's fax came in, but O'Rourke, receiving the message on his machine, was so impressed with Smith's letter that he quickly fired off this reply.

"It was a great letter," Smith recalls. "I requested the manuscript over the phone immediately. It resulted in a two-hardcover deal with Simon & Schuster at $100,000 apiece, with an additional $150,000 in bonus money attached to each title based on foreign sales performance and/or achievement of national best-seller status. Total deal: 500,000 dollars before paperback reprint sale. Publication is set for February 1996."

The Synopsis

If you accomplished what you should have with your query letter, the reader should be anxiously rummaging through your 9 × 12 envelope for the second half of your proposal—the synopsis. This is the final tease to close the sale; to induce the reader to ask for the book itself.

To do that, your synopsis should chronicle each and every chapter of your book, distilling the main events, characters, and plot twists as they occur and progress—including the ending, as I mentioned before. This is critical: *You must reveal the ending*—who lives, who dies, who marries whom, who did it, etc. Never tease: "If you want to know how it all turns out, I'll send you the manuscript." At this stage the agent or the editor needs to know that your plot and structure work; to do that she needs to know everything—and now. She doesn't have time to read the whole book to find out if you've resolved everything or not.

Even though your novel may be written in the third person, write your synopsis in the *first* person to give it a feeling of immediacy (more than one agent told me this). The text should be written in narrative, not outline, form and should mimic the language and style of your book. Don't hesitate to extract choice quotes, classic scenes, and descriptive pearls from your book; it's an effective way to enliven the text and keep it from sounding monotonous. Another way to keep the reader reading is to break up your synopsis into chapters, just as you do in your book. That's because it's easier to read than a continuous twenty-five-page block of text, it shows how well or poorly you understand pace and structure, and it indicates how much thought you've put into your chapter beginnings and endings.

To make your characters come alive to the reader, introduce them as you do in the book—with colorful entrances, brief quotes, or anecdotes. Avoid short, playbill-type portraits like: "Tom is a thirty-four-year-old Jamaican aerobics instructor, moody, bisexual, dabbles in the occult. . . ."

Instead, try to weave descriptions of your characters into the text like this:

> ". . . a man to whom the difference between a pasture and a meadow seemed important, who got excited about sky color, who wrote a little poetry but not much fiction. Who played the guitar, who earned his living by images and carried his tools in knapsacks. Who seemed like the wind. And moved like it. Came from

it, perhaps." (Robert James Waller describing Robert Kincaid in *The Bridges of Madison County*.)

As with nonfiction-book-proposal chapter summaries, condensing your five hundred-page novel down to a ten- or twenty-five-page synopsis may seem more daunting than writing the book—what do I leave in, what do I leave out? To you, every word and every scene is crucial: "I can't possibly include all the clues and red herrings! How can I describe the plot's nuances, the intricately shaded characters, the time period? How can I showcase my descriptive writing, my action, my dialogue?"

You can't. But know this: The agent or editor *knows* you can't. *She's* putting you under this restriction, not you. She knows it's not your fault; in fact, she's putting every other writer sending in a synopsis under the same constraint. All that's important to her is the big picture: the intrigue of the plot, the synergy of the structure, the realism of the characters, how it all comes together at the end. (I mentioned that you must reveal the ending, didn't I? I can't say this enough times.) In short, she's just looking at the major elements, where the most common problems occur, so she can screen out those projects with the obvious handicaps. Literary agent Sandra Watt of Sandra Watt and Associates in Hollywood, California, says she can tell what a writer's style is like from one page just as well as she can from ten pages.

So don't panic; just do the best you can and describe your book as accurately, completely, and dramatically as you can.

Total length of synopsis: ten to twenty-five pages (each chapter one to three pages).

Questions & Answers

Q: Is it true that the best time to send out a novel query is when your book's subject matter is "hot"?

A: I don't buy the notion that publishers look for certain genres at certain times, and I certainly don't recommend writing a book just to try to catch such a "wave." Oh, every once in a while a few big books on the same topic will hit the bestseller list at the same time (like the late eighties-early nineties "courtroom saga" era when Scott Turow's *Presumed Innocent* and *Burden of Proof* were followed by John Grisham's *The Firm, The Pelican Brief,* and *The Client*). But that's not a craze; it's a coincidence. If you don't believe me, browse through a few publishers' catalogs the next time you believe a "trend" is sweeping the publishing industry. You'll discover that 95 percent of the *other* books published by those and competing houses are the same ones they always publish: thrillers, mysteries, westerns, romance, science fiction, crime, horror; in short, a little bit of everything. For the most part, book publishers take what comes in when it comes in; they don't sit in their ivory towers and secretly decide: "Let's do only alien serial killers in 1995 and romantic westerns in 1996."

Q: I've heard many novels are sold with neither a query nor a synopsis. What's the deal with them?

A: Their writers never took "no" for an answer; i.e., they found other, more innovative ways of getting their feet in the door. It's the same way many screenwriters and TV writers break into *their* impossible-to-break-into industries—by complementing their querying with networking. By knowing, or finding a way to get to know, people who know an agent or an editor. Connections. Do you know anybody who has an agent or a book editor? Ask that person to pass your book on to her. Are there any local writers' conferences coming up? Agents and editors who attend such events are usually looking for material. In short, hustle.

One top New York agent admitted to me that much of the writing he sells comes to him from referrals, not queries. Manuscripts are passed to him from individuals who know someone who knows someone who knows him. These writers are dogmatic, incessant bloodhounds who use every means, every excuse, every contact available to track agents and editors down. They find a way.

One of the best examples I came across last year was from this March 1995 press release I received from Doubleday (underlines are mine):

> Enclosed is a copy of one of the most talked-about novels of the year—*The Standoff* by Chuck Hogan. There has been a steady buzz about this remarkable first novel ever since the manuscript first landed on the desk of Amanda Urban at ICM last spring.
>
> Almost on a lark, <u>Hogan sent his manuscript to Urban on the advice of a friend who had met her once at a cocktail party</u>. She was the only agent he contacted. Now, at the young age of twenty-six, Hogan has quickly become an instant star of both the publishing and Hollywood industries.
>
> Doubleday bought Hogan's debut novel in an intensely

heated two-day auction involving five major publishers. Within just a few weeks we had accepted a blockbuster six-figure paperback floor, movie rights had gone to New Line Cinema, and foreign rights had been sold to the UK, Italy, Holland, Germany, France, and Brazil.

Up until his novel was sold, Hogan was working as an assistant manager at a video store.

Q: You suggest pitching a novel by sending a query and a synopsis together. Why can't I send just a query?

A: I don't recommend this approach for two reasons. First, a query by itself is nowhere near as powerful of a first impression as a query and a synopsis—and you want your package to wow the reader. Second, sending only a query locks every novel submission you send out into an automatic three-stage affair (query, synopsis and sample chapters, book). Few agents or editors will ask for the whole book from just a one-page query; it happens, as my sample letters demonstrate, but it's rare. Sending a query and a synopsis together right off the bat, however, could reduce your submission process by one third (the reader may skip the sample chapters and go right to the book) because it's more complete, effective, and packs more wallup.

Q: You say I shouldn't query until my book's finished and ready to send out. The catch-22 is, I can't finish my novel until I do some expensive on-location research—and I can't afford to do that research until I get an advance. What's the harm in querying with what I've written so far? If a publisher likes my first three chapters, I may get an advance from that, which would allow me to do the research and finish the book.

A: I empathize with your situation because it's a difficult and common one that I experienced once myself. Approximately three years ago I finished the first draft of a new novel. Since I knew it would probably take months of querying and waiting and querying and waiting just to get one bite from an agent—and that's if I was lucky—I decided to start the query process even though the book was not yet in final form. In my naivete I figured by the time anyone responded, I would have most of the book—if not all of it—polished and ready to send out.

Four months later my dream came true: An agent returned one of my postcards asking to see the rest of the book. Just one problem. At that stage of my final rewrite, it dawned on me that my original protagonist was no longer working out. Not only had he steadfastly refused, after numerous attempts on my part, to jump into bed with the female sidekick I'd so graciously introduced him to (for specifically that reason, I might add), but he'd turned into a lout. So I'd decided to ditch him.

Wouldn't you know it, just when I get the potential break of a lifetime, just when an agent finally wants to see *my* book, to read *my* story, to start negotiations with publishers over *my* six-figure advance, I have to tell her that . . . er, uh . . . remember that book you liked, the one featuring the lout? Well, heh-heh, it's history—and so is he. How about if I interest you in this other angle I came up with. . . . ?"

Because this change caused me to have to redo the entire book from scratch at that point—with all new characters, scenes, directions, and complications—I was essentially back at the *first*-draft stage, not the final one. Too ashamed to explain what had really happened, I wrote the agency back and said, "Sorry, but I'm not quite ready to send you the rest at this time." A year later, when I finally was ready, I sent the agent a note asking if she was still interested. She politely declined. Once you get an agency or a publisher salivating to see the rest of your book, they want it *now*, not six months or a year later.

Novels are unpredictable, they take sudden twists and turns. The characters you create evolve into living, breathing people who will do and say what *they* want, not what you want. Therefore, you won't know for certain, until you write the final word of your final draft, where your book is truly heading and when it's truly done. That's why I suggest you tough out the early hardships the best way you can and query only after you've finished.

CHAPTER SEVEN

The Cover Letter

"You will have written exceptionally well if, by skillful arrangement of your words, you have made an ordinary one seem original."
Horace

Some manuscripts can be—in fact, *should be*—sent in cold, with no pre-approval or OK from an editor beforehand. These are fiction (short stories), humor, essays, opinion pieces, poetry, jokes and fillers, reprints, and newspaper articles. But you're not off the hook completely; these forms of writing still need a cover letter to accompany them. It's tacky to send just a story and an SASE, with no explanation of what it is, who you are, or why you sent it to that person specifically. So in this chapter we will discuss what cover letters are, why they're important, and how to write good ones.

What a Cover Letter Is

A cover letter is not really a letter; it's a note (no more than three paragraphs in length) whose sole purpose is to briefly introduce yourself and your submission, then get out of the way. You know your cover letter works when the reader sets it aside quickly to get to your story. *It serves no other function.*

The key word is brevity. If a query letter should be no more than a page or a page-and-a-half in length, a cover letter should be no more than a half page. Your manuscript is the star of this submission, not the cover letter. Therefore, you don't need to open with a great lead, create a "hook," or play with different letter formats to catch the editor's eye. Neither is this the place to hype your manuscript, explain how much work you put into the story, recite your resume, or show off your new 3-D embossed letterhead.

Your cover letter gives an editor an immediate image of you and demonstrates how you communicate, how you think, and how you conduct business. If your letter impresses an editor, that positive feeling will hopefully spill over into the reading of your article (it might be read less critically). A good cover letter does this to me. If I get a neat, clean, no-nonsense cover letter, I feel confident and secure that what's attached (your manuscript) is probably going to be worth my time to read. I haven't read one word of your story, yet I'm already looking forward to it. I will read it more carefully and seriously than if your cover letter were poor, and I'll be less prone to discard it quickly. In short, a good cover letter can earn your manuscript respect. All because of three simple paragraphs. It's amazing what a little extra time and effort on your part can do to assuage a busy reader. And in this business, you need every break you can get.

By contrast, a rambling, unprofessional, poorly written letter—or no cover letter at all—gives the impression that you have little regard for the quality of your work—and may cause an editor to give your manuscript the skim treatment: scanning it for the slightest excuse to reject it based on her negative reaction to your cover letter. "Aha, I *knew* it wasn't going to be any good." In his book, *175 High-Impact Cover Letters*, Richard II. Beatty advises job applicants on the importance of cover letters accompanying resumes. His job-search principles could just as easily apply, however, to the importance of cover letters accompanying manuscripts: "I have never ceased to be amazed at the fact that some people will put hours (or even days) into the preparation and design of the 'perfect' resume—one that impressively highlights their qualifications and skillfully markets their credentials—then put only five minutes preparation time into a cover letter that causes them to fall flat on their face. Such behavior simply defies all logic and rules of common sense."

A good cover letter consists of three sections, arranged in separate paragraphs. In order, they are:

1. **The introductory paragraph** (describes what you're enclosing and why).
2. **The biographical paragraph** (explains a little about yourself).
3. **The concluding paragraph** (politely closes the letter).

The Introductory Paragraph

The first 'graph should come right to the point. Simply state what you've sent. ("I'm enclosing an essay, 'A Letter To My Son,' for your consideration.") Small talk, a clever lead, any other introductory folderol is neither appropriate nor anticipated in cover-letter commencements.

Next say something, in the same paragraph, about your article in a few sentences. ("It is a letter I penned to my five-year-old adopted son while he was literally in the air on the way to meet me from Thailand ten years ago. I waited until this year to present it to him, until I was sure he was mature enough to understand the emotions—worry, joy, fear, and hope—I was feeling on the eve of his beatific entrance into my life.") The reader doesn't want a treatise on your story, just a telegram. Remember, you're not trying to coax the reader into sending away for the piece—it's already enclosed. You're just labelling what you've delivered.

And finally, conclude the first paragraph by telling why you sent it to that particular individual and/or publication. ("I sent it to you because all the readers of *Adoption Quarterly* have at one time experienced—or will experience the same chords of emotion that I did prior to meeting my new son for the first time. For that reason, my article could serve as a catharsis for your readers because I have put down into words the sentiments they may yearn to say to *their* adopted child one day.")

End your first paragraph here. Bite your lip if you have to, but end it. Don't go on and on just because you've got more room. Any element you add to your opening 'graph at this point will dilute your cover letter's effectiveness and reduce the chances of your manuscript being read favorably.

The Biographical Paragraph

In your second paragraph briefly chronicle your writing experience and what you've published that's relevant or similar to your story. ("I have published a half dozen other essays dealing with children or adoption for such publications as *Parents Magazine*, *Newsday*, and *Reader's Digest*.") If you've published nothing, if what you have published is dissimilar to what you're currently proposing, or if the publications you've been published in are vastly inferior to the one you're submitting this manuscript to, simply say nothing.

Conclude this paragraph by outlining any expertise and/or background you have that's relevant to your story or subject matter. ("I bring a bounty of insight into this piece because not only have I adopted my own child but both my wife and I have volunteered for the last seven years at various local orphanages and international adoption agencies.") Again, say nothing if you have no pertinent experience.

Sample Letters

Dear Mr. Wood:

The enclosed outline is presented for your consideration. A brief introduction:

My credits include more than twelve hundred articles, fifteen nonfiction books, a half-dozen television documentaries, and numerous "ghosted" pieces. In addition, I've been a contributor, staff writer, and roving editor for *Reader's Digest* since 1967.

My association with the *Digest* ended recently—leaving me free once again to work with other magazines. As a "born-again freelancer" I'm convinced I can find and deliver articles that will appeal to your readers. Many thanks for your consideration.

Sincerely,

Stanley L. Englebardt

P.S. Enclosed are reprints of some of my *Digest* articles.

COMMENTS

Obviously, twelve hundred articles and fifteen books would catch any editor's eye, but it was his brevity and matter-of-factness about his experience that impressed me. He isn't boasting or condescending; he simply states the obvious, laying out his entire life's work in two sentences. In addition, his tone is light and conversational, making an editor feel it would be easy and fun to work with him. He doesn't describe his article, though, which would have made his letter even better. But I guess when you've accumulated this many credits, you know—and so does the editor—that the enclosed story will be read (which it was).

Dear Mr. Wood,

Enclosed is *Table 64*, a humor piece about my extraordinary adventures on the *Queen Elizabeth 2* crossing to France. It was all impossible and yet it all happened; how I slept in second class but ate in first next to William F. Buckley, Walter Cronkite, and Bob Hope; how I sailed with only three days notice; how I lived a moment every woman dreams.

At fifty I decided to begin living the last three lines of the poem, *When I Am an Old Woman*: ". . . maybe I ought to practice a little now? So people who know me are not too shocked and surprised when suddenly I am old and start to wear purple."

Every woman will journey with me through the celebrity-filled dining room in my red dress, dine with me next to British nobility, and dream with me about high society.

Since my fiftieth birthday I have journeyed to Russia for a month-long archeological dig, taken up tap dancing, had a dozen former CIA operatives to dinner, conquered my fears from a dependent childhood and travelled to New York alone, hiked a mountain, and will soon audition to dance in *42nd Street*. I will live my second fifty years free.

There is a red dress in every woman. *Table 64* will let her wear it with me.

I look forward to your response.

Sincerely,

Paula Spellman

COMMENTS

This is the kind of letter that really makes you want to read what's enclosed. I didn't know this woman, but after reading this cover letter I liked her, respected her, and *wanted* to like what she'd written. She speaks directly to our readers and our magazine. Instead of stating "Enclosed is a humor piece entitled blah-blah," which would have been proper to do, she goes one step further and teases the reader about the piece. Instead of listing her credits, she paints a colorful picture of her life. She exudes passion for her piece without overdoing it, a difficult feat.

Dear Mr. Wood:

    Normally, I don't admit to perusing *Cosmopolitan* but, really, when standing in line at the Big Bear (our grocery store), it is about the best offering. I noticed that *Cosmo* had an article about indecisiveness, the trauma of decision-making, so, since I was making a decision about a job offer, I bought the magazine. Later that night, still feeling undecided about the job, I read my Gemini horoscope. No help. I leafed through the magazine and found the "On My Mind" page, read an essay about being neurotic over one's hair, and then another titled "Old Men Can't Jump." I fell asleep a bit later and had a dream that Walter Matthau, the late Don Ameche, and George Burns were part of the new Celtics basketball team.

    The next morning I awoke and wrote this thing I call "You Say You Busted Lillian Hellman?" It's an all-too-true personal and uncensored response.

    What can I say? Columbus is gloomy and full of dirty snow.

Sincerely,

Nancy Dillon

COMMENTS

If this letter seems too informal and stylish, you're right; it would be inappropriate to use with an editor you're approaching for the first time. But this writer had already written a cover story for us and had corresponded with the editor many times. I only include it to show how you can take a few more liberties with editors once you're familiar with them (plus I loved it). This woman writes great letters, and her letter style is the same as her article style. As she put it to me: "I always try to write everything as if I were writing a letter to someone I liked. If I think of my writing as a letter to a friend, it frees me to be myself and takes away the fear and uncertainty. It's a good way to get past that dreaded inertia." This kind of teaser put me into the right frame of mind to jump into the story (in this case the accompanying article was equally funny and offbeat). But again, I recommend this approach only if you already know an editor.

Questions & Answers

Q: Is it ever appropriate to preface a *query* with a cover letter?

A: It's not necessary, but more and more writers are doing it. It takes more effort on your part, but it also has some pluses.

On the plus side, a cover letter accompanying a query letter essentially divides your query into two neat and distinct parts: Part I being the cover letter (which states what is enclosed, why the subject's important, where and how the article could be used in the magazine, your qualifications and background, etc.) and Part II being the article idea itself. This allows you to separate the "business and personal" part of your query from your actual article description. This can be a godsend—no more having to cram all that info together onto one page!

Introducing your query with a cover letter also makes your presentation more formal, polite, and professional than it already may be. It allows you more space in the cover letter for addenda ("Photos are available . . ." "Here are some other angles to the story . . ." "I really enjoyed your last issue . . ." "Your co-editor Franklin, whom I've sold a couple of articles to in the past, suggested I send this to you . . ."). But most of all, enclosing a cover letter lets you devote an entire page to your article idea. This luxury can really come in handy if your proposed article is a complicated project to explain.

On the negative side, adding a cover letter is obviously more time consuming for both you and the editor: You have to write two letters instead of one each time you query an editor; it's that much more stuff for the editor to read, and it's one more piece of paper to potentially separate and misplace. My gut reaction? Cover letters with queries aren't necessary; you can do without them 95 percent of the time. But this is your call here, not mine: Do you want to expend the extra time and energy?

Q: You say certain forms of writing—fiction, humor, essays, etc.—never require a query, but you never explain why.

A: That's because these delicate genres, unlike nonfiction articles, can't be fixed if they're written poorly. (How can an editor rewrite what can only come from the writer's head, voice, and style?) Since no query has yet been devised to assure an editor, with the same degree of certainty that a nonfiction query can, that a writer—no matter what his track record—can deliver a publishable short story, humor article, essay, poem, etc., an editor would be unwise to assign one. Hence, query letters are superfluous.

Nonfiction, on the other hand, is more formulaic and, thus, more flexible to work with. Even if everything goes wrong with a nonfiction article, it can often be salvaged by an editor—by rearranging information, rewriting a lead, excising quotes, adding new experts, juicing up the ending, etc. It's like flower arranging: just shuffle the stems and leaves around until it looks OK.

But fiction, humor, poetry—and to a lesser extent, essays and opinion pieces—are another species altogether. They are a kaleidoscope of images and ideas and characters that spring impulsively from the writer's imagination. How can an editor rewrite (or envision) what a writer improvised (or would improvise)? These types of writing are like oil paintings *of* a flower arrangement. Try fixing *that*.

CHAPTER EIGHT

Other Correspondence

> *"Letters of thanks, letters from banks,*
> *Letters of joy from girl and boy,*
> *Receipted bills and invitations*
> *To inspect new stock or to visit relations,*
> *And applications for situations,*
> *And timid lovers' declarations,*
> *And gossip, gossip from all the nations."*
> W.H. Auden

I'm sorry, but there *is* correspondence beyond the query and cover letter. Lots of it. Once you make a few sales and start to get more assignments, you'll find yourself writing to editors constantly—not to mention publishers, agents, authorities, celebrities, publicists, PR agencies, organizations, etc. This chapter will explain many of the common types of miscellaneous letters you will be called upon to write—and write well—during your career.

The chapter is divided into two sections. The first part includes letters you will most commonly write to editors: assignment-acceptance letters, follow-up letters, negotiation letters, update letters, rewrite letters, etc. The second part includes letters you will most often write to people other than editors: request-for-interview letters, request-for-information letters, introduction letters, etc.

Although none of these missives are as essential as the almighty duo that comprise the title of this book, they will nevertheless constitute the bulk of your day-to-day freelance-related correspondence. Therefore, if you want to communicate clearly and effectively with your peers, clients, and potential clients, don't take this chapter lightly. How you write the seemingly routine and inconsequential letters that follow will represent to the literary world how you conduct business.

Letters Between You and Editors

The vast majority of your freelance-related writing will be directed to newspaper, magazine, and/or book editors. Obviously, there isn't enough room to incorporate *every* conceivable letter you might write an editor, so I've only presented the most common and useful types, featuring actual letters to illustrate each example.

As you gain experience, you'll learn that no assignment is ever the same. One assignment may not require any of these letters. The next one may demand all of them, and many more besides. It all depends on the nature and difficulty of the assignment, your relationship with the editor or agent, and a host of other factors. Use the sample letters on the following pages to help guide you through various situations and to help inspire you through the day-to-day business—and maze—of freelance writing.

"How Do I Deliver a Manuscript To an Editor?"

You've gotten the assignment, finished the piece, and are putting it in the envelope. Should you send the article with nothing else? Should you attach a Post-it note ("Here's the article. Thanks for the assignment. Call if any questions.")? Should you write a cover letter?

Send a letter. Take the extra step, as a professional courtesy and as a safeguard, to at least explain the contents of your submission and make sure what the editor receives is what you enclosed.

Dear Mr. Wood:

Here is:

1) a diskette with the interview. It's called "Uweint," it's written in Xywrite, and the intro is at the top.

2) a copy of the transcript of the entire interview. You'll note I did a first edit on the beginning of this; then I gave up and went right to the disk.

3) the bill from the transcript service. Other expenses (they're not many; lunch for Reinhardt and phone bills) will follow when they're complete.

Thanks again for the opportunity. It was fun. Obviously I'm always available for questions and more editing, and I warned Reinhardt we'd probably need to contact him again. Please call when you've received this so I know it arrived safely.

Sincerely,

Julie Rovner

COMMENTS

This letter accompanied Rovner's disk and manuscript of her assigned interview with health economist Uwe Reinhardt that we published in our November-December 1994 issue. It describes what the package contains, includes some pertinent information, and ends with a polite and reassuring note. Just right. An editor doesn't need a two-page explanatory letter, nor does she want a manuscript with not so much as a "hello" from the writer either.

Contrary to popular belief, this is *not* the time to pitch another idea to the editor. Some overly ambitious writers tag onto such letters: "Now that this assignment's out of the way, I've got another idea right down your alley. . . ." Withstand the urge to ride this wave all the way to the shore. There's plenty of time for that later. The poor editor hasn't even read your manuscript yet, let alone worked with you during its various rewriting/editing/fact-checking production stages. The best time to pitch an editor with another query is when she and the staff are abuzz with excitement after the issue featuring your article hits the newsstands. That's the most euphoric time of the month for magazine editors: The finished copies have just arrived, everyone's oohing and ahhing and congratulating themselves, the industry is just getting wind of what they've done, and feedback from readers and peers are starting to stream in. *That's* when you want to send a note, slap your editor on the back, and say, "Congratulations on a great-looking issue! Don't you think it's time we did this again?"

Dear Mr. Wood:

Enclosed are:

1) 3.5 disk formatted for WordPerfect 5.0

2) Interview transcripts

3) Hard copy of proposed interview, approx. 4,000 words

4) Copy of Angela Lambert interview with Jessica Mitford from *The Independent*, London, 09/21/93.

There is sufficiently good material to both entertain and inform your audience. I was heartened to find that Angela Lambert, in her interview with Mitford, corroborates exactly my experience with her once I arrived in London and, likely, the difficulties encountered by the transcriptionist in understanding her English. Although Ms. Mitford was gracious about being interviewed, she had, in the intervening time, made new commitments once she arrived in London. This included a 900-word weekly column (for four weeks) for *The Times of London* (three topics at 300 words apiece). As a consequence, these new commitments, coupled with her jet lag and, of course, her age, encroached upon our interview time.

Ms. Mitford has given me permission to quote liberally, where necessary, from her books in the interest of accuracy, especially concerning names, dates, and places. For three questions I have added minimal phrases to frame the material, appropriately, for the reader. In no way does this alter Ms. Mitford's comments nor her intent.

For two questions regarding both Harry Truman and Paul Robeson in which she gave incomplete responses, I have referred to her second memoir, *A Fine Old Conflict*; and for the final question regarding the creation of a Jessica Mitford model casket, I referred to her journalism anthology, *Poison Penmanship: The Gentle Art of Muckraking*. In the interview, Mitford says she received a letter from a Midwestern manufacturer. However, in her book, she says she received "plans and specifications."

Without access to dictation equipment, I have had to rely on secretarial services in both London and Boston. You will find sections of the transcripts frustrating. Both had considerable difficulty with Ms. Mitford's upper-class English accent, especially the London transcriptionist, which illustrates how the English have a historically demarcated class distinction. In spite of more than a half-century of living in America, Mitford, despite her leftist leanings, retains the demeanor and accent of the social class to which she was born. Luckily, I had little difficulty understanding her. Therefore, I was able to go back to the tapes to clarify gaps and spaces listed as "inaudible."

I will be sending along a photograph and biographical comments next week. As well, I will include the bills for the transcriptionist in London, for the John Pearson book mentioned in the manuscript, and some taxi receipts.

Thank you for assigning me the interview.
Yours sincerely,
Joseph Dumas

COMMENTS

This is an excellent example of how to brief an editor about your project—especially if it was a particularly massive and difficult one. This writer described what he sent and what was coming, and provided important information about certain elements and obstacles that had occurred. When I read the piece, I was informed and up-to-date about all that had transpired.

Ideal C   "How Do I Thank an Editor?"

...ceive kudos; bylines belong—deservedly so—to writers. Our pleasure mainly
...g that a story we worked on was the best it could be, was read with interest by
...as an enjoyable and agreeable collaboration with the writer. A short, simple
...appreciative writer, therefore, can make an editor's week and endear you to her

...warrant a thank-you letter? Since any such note can bond a relationship, you
...many! If you're unsure, though, ask yourself if you would ever be critical of a
...n from someone you didn't like. Here are four things to remember with thank-

1.

> Samuel Page
> *Everyone's Magazine*
> 1515 Fifth Avenue
> New York, NY 10001
>
> Dear Mr. Page:

...y. If you're thanking an editor for the work she did on your article, send your
...the issue appears.
...y what you're grateful for and why it pleased you:

2.

> Enclosed is my short story, 'A Christmas Ta...
> ous twist on the fabled holiday classic, usin...
> ters instead of human ones. I feel it will ap...
> young readers of your pet magazine. (In ca...
> fused, the odd character names are anagram...
> Oliver Twist characters).

...you for the work you did."
...k you for the painless 1,200-word cut I understand you had to make just
...icle went to press—I can't even tell where the cuts were made!"

3.

> My work has appeared in several children's...
> cations including *Jack and Jill*, *Highlights f...
> *Pets Magazine*. My children's book, *A Dog...
> currently in its third printing.

...re note to thanking the person. Don't combine it with anything else (query,
...etc.).
...related comment (promise to meet the editor the next time you're in town, say
...bout the publication or a mutual acquaintance, etc.).

4.

> Thank you for your time and attention. I l...
> hearing from you.

1.

> Sincerely,
>
> Deborah Penword
>
> Enclosure:
>   Short story, "A Christmas Tail"
>   SASE

Dear John,

I've been meaning to write to let you know how pleased I am with the way you and *Modern Maturity* handled my four pieces. Thanks to a good job on your end I have to admit I'm pretty proud of the way the quartet turned out. The summer essay, especially.

I've rewritten each of the essays, and I'd like to find either a publisher with a good art department or a photographer who specializes in farm and ranch and rural landscapes to create a book with the essays as text.

While fencing this spring I ran across some of the cedar fence posts I mentioned in the fall fencing piece, the ones my granddad dated with a hammer and punch. So by way of saying thanks for taking on my work (and treating my work with care), here's a memento from the Beer Ranch on Jackson Creek.

I hope we'll get the chance to work together again someday, John.

Best of luck,

Ralph Beer

COMMENTS

If I accomplish nothing else in my career, I will know because of this simple, four-paragraph note that the synergy I experienced with one notable writer—Montana novelist and essayist Ralph Beer—was a very special one. And we *will* work again someday. The fence post he sent me is still in my office.

SIONAL

tenets apply here as
nandment One for
rs. This writer ad-
letter to the correct
le sure the editor's
ablication's name and
e correct, formalized
n, kept her letterhead
:d and spell-checked
id enclosed an SASE.

UCTORY
PH

d opening paragraph.
ll the necessary infor-
editor needs without
word. Sometimes, as
you may need to ex-
:o read, interpret, or
nuscript. This writer
:nthetical note to clar-
ng the editor would
ow when reading his

PHICAL
PH

deal paragraph briefly
writer's relevant cred-
would launch into a lit-
ything he'd done and
he'd worked. Don't

DING PARAGRAPH

innocuous statements
closes to almost any
. They're polite with-
submissive; expectant
ng pushy.

"How Do I Follow-up With an Editor?"

During the course of a typical assignment, you may need to drop a note to your editor for a number of reasons: to have her send you additional material, to revise or confirm an earlier correspondence, to answer or ask a question, to remind her of something you need or will provide, to inform her of changes you're making, or to simply give a status report about your project. In short, just about anything that will spread good will, instill confidence, and reassure the editor that all is going well—or if it isn't, that you're on top of it but need some input before proceeding.

Here are two such letters. The first one is an assignment update from novelist and former *New York Times* political columnist Tom Wicker prior to his April-May 1994 interview with Gore Vidal. The second one is from *Los Angeles Times* film-critic-at-large Sheila Benson regarding the rewrite on her interview with playwright and screenwriter Horton Foote.

Dear Mr. Wood:

I delayed signing the enclosed contracts and returning them to you until I had things settled with Gore Vidal, which now has been done. Due to some scheduling conflicts with him, I've had to schedule the trip a bit later than I would have liked but I hope early enough for your purposes.

I will leave New York on Tuesday, July 20, reaching Naples via Frankfurt about noon Wednesday. Vidal will have someone meet and take me to his house and I plan to do the interview that day and probably the next. I'll be back in the U.S. the following week and will hope to have the text in your hands fairly early in August.

On Vidal's advice, I booked my flight with Lufthansa, which has a convenient Naples flight out of Frankfurt. I don't have the exact fare but it will be considerably under four thousand dollars; and I expect to make the entire trip (will be chargeable to you) within your stated budget.

Most of the time between June 10 and July 20, I will be at my farm in Vermont; you should try to reach me there first.

No doubt one of us should call the other as July 20 approaches, for final consultations on this interesting assignment. But please let me know right away if anything in these arrangements doesn't suit. I'll try to make any changes necessary.

Sincerely,

Tom Wicker

COMMENTS

This letter didn't need to be sent (I never mandated an update), but editors will kill for writers like this. How long do such notes take to send off? Minutes. How long do such notes linger in the recipient's mind? Years. Wicker is a southern gentlemen from the old school who felt obliged to keep me abreast of his goings-on at various stages of this potentially difficult long-distance project. It's this kind of professional courtesy that instills confidence and loyalty—and future assignments.

Dear John:

Your computer should have this safely by now, but since, alas, neither bold nor italics travel computer to computer, I am also sending you a paper copy in the hope that the changes jump out at you easily. (I may even highlight them; let me take one last look and see if it's clear without the highlighting or not.)

You'll see a lot fuller answers to some of the questions you had; I think they're very interesting. General questions, about descriptions of the South, for example, he didn't answer for the reasons provided: He feels "the South," per se, is a cliché. He also feels the description of his father's store at the time he was growing up is a self-contained example of just what his part of the South *was* like.

This expanded version is about it for what we are going to get Horton to comment on. As I made notes to you within the text, this is an *extremely* private man, generous and expansive on every matter pertaining to work and even to areas of his family. But he will not comment any more about his wife's death or his private feelings about that than he has already—and very frankly, I don't think he should be hounded to. (Not that he could be; when that curtain comes down, it is *down*.) This is a man, for all his contemporaneousness, of another generation, with a sincere reverence for the privacy of certain parts of one's life and others' deaths.

Obviously, I'll be most interested in how this new material, and my own slight rearrangement of the text in one place, strikes you.

And as soon as I can get the Tab feature of my computer to stop frustrating me, I'll send along the expenses. And if I don't master it, you'll get the sections in longhand. Aargh!

With very warmest wishes,

Sheila Benson

COMMENTS

This was a tricky interview assignment because we had asked Benson in her rewrite to probe further, if possible, into some delicate areas during a sensitive time for Mr. Foote, whom she was interviewing for us. Her reply was detailed and informative, not to mention a wonderful read. She starts light, gets down to business, then ends light. She gives concise but clear and telling reasons for why she wasn't able to get all that we asked for.

"How Do I Say 'No' to an Editor?"

Writers are the ones who normally send out query letters, but editors also send many themselves. We're constantly on the prowl for new writers, for "name" writers, for writers whose styles match a particular project we're working on. You may be gratified to know that editors get rejected, too—a lot. If you're a beginning writer, you may not conceive of a situation where you would (1) ever get such an offer, or (2) if you did, turn it down! But it's always possible that the timing or the subject matter of an assignment pitched to you by an editor may be inappropriate for you. The key is how to say "no" to the invitation while still keeping the door open for future projects.

Turning somebody down is in some ways harder on paper than it is in person. That's because a "No, thank you" letter is more limited than a face-to-face "No, thank you." The receiver can't see your facial expressions, hear your tone of voice, ask a question, or clear up any misunderstandings. Therefore, your letter must be crystal clear and its manner as tactful and understanding as possible.

First, thank the person for the request. Second, say "No thanks" and express your regret at having to decline. Third, close pleasantly with a wish to participate next time (if you truly do). Avoid excuses and apologies; they aren't convincing. And don't lie or ascribe your refusal to someone else's actions. You're under no obligation to defend or explain the reason for your decision. Here are two that did the trick:

Dear John,

Thanks for your letter of 6/28. I'm always in the mood to read kind words about my writing.

Things here have been hectic, and I see no breathing space until August 25 or so. Right now, I'm dashing for a plane to New Mexico where I will be underground, exploring a cave for *National Geographic*.

After that I am home for a while. Perhaps we could explore article ideas over the phone at that time.

Sorry for the haste, but let's talk after I get back.

Sincerely,

Tim Cahill

Dear John Wood:

Thanks for your friendly letter. God knows, your twenty-two million is an impressive readership, an enviable audience, and my own parents are among that number.

As for my own work, though: I'm overcommitted on magazine assignments and scrambling to meet deadlines while trying to keep my current book project on track.

Maybe sometime in the future I'll have an idea that's right for you, and time to do it.

Best,

David Quammen

COMMENTS

Both are polite "Not right now, but thanks" letters that clearly imply the writers are interested and to try again. I did try again because Cahill, author of *Jaguars Ripped My Flesh*, *Pecked to Death by Ducks*, and others is one of the funniest adventure writers around; and Quammen, longtime nature columnist for *Outside* magazine, is one of the nation's best essayists. We're still working on story ideas.

"How Do I Say 'Yes' to an Editor?"

An editor has approached you about a possible assignment. How do you say, "I do!" in your reply? That might sound like a no-brainer, but just saying "Yes" sometimes can be tricky. You want to sound eager but not overanxious; interested but not desperately interested.

Just be cool. Express your intent to take on the assignment, but do so with composed formality. No exclamation points. No profuse thank yous. No sincere but deadly boners such as, "By giving me my first break, you've given me new hope and resolve you won't regret it!" *If you're a novice, don't blow your cover here*. In short, respond as if being offered an assignment is a common occurrence.

Dear Mr. Wood:

Thanks for your call about possibly doing an interview with Uwe Reinhardt for *Modern Maturity*. As I told you on the phone, I would be very interested in such an undertaking.

As you asked, I have enclosed several clips so you can get an idea of my work. Let me assure you that in addition to being an expert on health policy, I have also freelanced for a wide variety of publications—from *Better Homes & Gardens* and *Ladies' Home Journal* to *Grolier's Encyclopedia Americana*—and pride myself on being able to adapt to any style of writing.

Please let me know if you need anything else. If you can't reach [name omitted], you can also call [name omitted] or [name omitted] in the AARP federal affairs office in Washington, who I'm confident will vouch for my competence on this subject.

Thanks again for the opportunity.

Sincerely,

Julie Rovner

COMMENTS

Halfway through an assigned interview on health-care reform with health economist Uwe Reinhardt in 1994, our writer fizzled on the project and I had to scramble around to find another interviewer. The *Washington Post* was a good place to look because it often runs in-depth—and readable—health-policy articles, and someone suggested Julie Rovner, who often writes for it. I called her. She seemed interested in the rush project, but I wanted to know a little more about her. This was her reply.

The understated tone in Rovner's note is precisely the kind to earn an editor's trust: The writer neither oversells nor undersells, and she comes across professional and confident. In her case, she *is* a seasoned pro, but my point is, *any* writer writing a letter like this will come off as professional. In two or three brief paragraphs, she expresses her interest, outlines her qualifications, and even name-drops a few heavyweights in my organization who she knew would get my attention. I called them and they did indeed give her glowing recommendations. Her interview appeared in our November-December 1994 issue.

"How Do I Complain to an Editor— or Respond to a Complaint From an Editor?"

Not all assignments go smoothly, as all writers and editors can attest. There may come a time in your writer-editor relationship when conflict will arise or feelings will be upset. Disagreement and gripes are to be expected, but how you handle them will affect your future dealings with that person. Therefore, you must be careful to treat all such situations as just what they are—and nothing more.

If you're the one complaining, the most effective way to voice it is to (1) state what it is you're upset about, (2) give reasons for your stand (using as many anecdotes, facts, or witnesses you can), (3) state clearly the outcome you want, and (4) close with an upbeat request for an acceptable solution and for continued positive relations.

If you're responding to an editor's complaint, the best rule of thumb is: Do you still want to do business with this person and this publication? If you don't, if the editor's tone was rude, and if you're mad as hell, then fire off a "Same to you!" letter and be done with it. On the other hand, if you do want to work with the editor and the publication again and the editor's letter was constructive and polite (although still utterly wrong in your opinion), then here's what to do:

1. Before you dash off your response, think and stay calm. Read the letter carefully to make sure you haven't overreacted or misunderstood the tone and/or purpose of the letter. The last thing you want to do is react to something the editor never actually wrote—or did write but didn't mean what you think she meant.

2. Decide what you want your letter to achieve and then state your position clearly: Do you want to apologize? to rebut? to work out a compromise? to tell her to take a hike? to exchange lawyers' phone numbers? Once you set your course, keep to it and don't ramble.

3. Summarize up front the issue at hand, even though both parties know what it is. This will allay the other person's fears (always a concern) that you might not have "gotten" it and that you do indeed understand her side.

4. Keep your letter factual and dispassionate. Being sarcastic or abusive may feel great, but it won't help you achieve your objective. Put yourself in the editor's place. Would such a tone make her more cooperative? The more focused and collected you are, the more you will be assured of being heard and avoid shaming the other person. Don't just say, "You're being unfair." Say, "I believe it's unfair to accuse me of running up expenses when you never told me what my limit was."

5. Close the letter by wishing for a mutually agreeable solution, and state that you look forward to continuing your pleasant relations. Remember, how you handle this communication will greatly affect subsequent assignments with that editor and magazine.

Below is a letter sent to me by our contributing travel editor, Charles Barnard, concerning a contract dispute.

Dear John,

First off, many thanks for your kind remarks about my Newfoundland piece. I enjoyed going there (always do) and I enjoyed writing the story, so perhaps that's what comes through. But you know, we writers sit back here in our dank caves and send forth our efforts, often into a void. Actors are the first to say that applause is the nourishment on which they thrive—but what do writers live on? (Cedar shavings from the pencil sharpener.) So your applause is very, very welcome. It's the first I've had on the piece.

Now then, on to other business.

I'm sorry to have to return the contract to you herewith unsigned, but as the editor will confirm, I do not sign contracts (anywhere) that contain the notorious "hold harmless" clauses. Even the contracts I sign for my travel pieces for you, innocuous as they may be from a legal point of view, do not contain this clause.

I was once sued for 7 million dollars by a guy whose name I spelled Levy—and whose name was Leavey. The fact checkers at the publisher didn't catch it. Leavey, an Irishman, said he had been portrayed as a Jew—and, in the context of an anecdote, as a cowardly Jew at that. Of course, it was all nonsense, but I had liens slapped on everything I owned while the publisher turned his back on me and said, "Sorry, buddy, you signed a 'hold harmless' agreement with us, so defend yourself the best you can." It took a couple of years and no little expense to get out from under that.

It only takes one lesson of that sort in life.

All best,

Charles

COMMENTS

You almost have to read this letter twice to realize the writer is complaining about something! The writer starts off with a compliment and some polite chitchat, then gets down to business. He states his problem, what action he's taking, and outlines his reasons for doing so. In addition, he helps the editor understand his action by weaving in a colorful anecdote illustrating where he's coming from. He's firm but calm. The matter is strictly business with him. Even if I had disagreed with him, I would have been hardpressed to lose my temper over this letter (and did not).

"How Do I Respond To an Inquiry From an Editor?"

There are many things an editor may ask of you—far too many to list here—but here are a couple. The first one below is from a writer whose article was sent to me by her writing teacher—and not a bad one, I might add: novelist and essayist William Kittredge, a Professor of English and Creative Writing at the University of Montana. Kittredge said the writer had several stories but wanted me to see this one first. I was overwhelmed by her article and fought a long, two-month battle with my superiors to publish it, to no avail. I finally called her up and explained that the phone call was one of the most difficult ones I'd ever had to make in my editing career: I had to turn down a piece I thought was one of the best I'd ever read. Then I asked if she could send me one of her other articles. This letter was her reply.

Dear John:

I'm still luxuriating in your words of praise yesterday on the phone for my piece, "Widow Making." Already I'm starting to figure I made up the whole conversation, both my part and yours. Thanks so very much for liking my work, for going to bat for it, and for recounting to me in such detail the course of its warm initial reception on through its eventual rejection.

Emboldened by your assessment, I'll take a deep breath and ship it off to either *Harper's* or the *New Yorker*. Good heavens.

Meanwhile, here's my "Lumbering with Jack." You alerted me that, at almost 5,400 words, it is much too long. But if you think it has merit, there might be a way to whittle it down.

I have another piece underway. It's about being from the Bay Area and playing Missoula's personal ads, an indoor sport which has, so far, provided me a fair amount of downside color, but not much upside (though I did meet a man I liked pretty well until he invited me to his place for elkburgers, thereby affording me a chance to peruse his personal library. His only hardback book was titled *The Lie: Evolution*).

Thanks very, very much for your encouragement and your generous praise. I savor your words, and am sustained by them.

Sincerely,

Helen Joyce Harris

COMMENTS

Her letter does so much—it is emotional yet business-like, humorous yet pithy, terse yet vivid. And it all reads so effortlessly. Remember this writer's name.

The second letter below shows how to respond when an editor needs additonal information. It is rare for an assigned article to come in pristine, with nary a peep out of an editor. Most of the time she will have at least a few concerns: It needs some more research, another question or two asked of the main subject, a statistic clarified for the fact-checker, additional rewriting, or whatever.

Obviously, the most important thing you must do is to reply to everything the editor requests, or if you can't, explain why. Then end the letter. Don't clutter it with other stuff or you may forget what it was the editor asked for in the first place. It's nerve-wracking for me, especially during deadline time, to get back a reply from a writer and find he only addressed two of the three things I had frantically asked for. This is a good example of how to respond when an editor beckons.

Dear John,

Thanks for your very kind words. I'm glad everybody liked the new interview. Working for appreciative journalists and editors is a gratifying experience.

I've rewritten the intro to account for the problems—and to make it generally better. Have a look.

No problem with Bennett seeming to take a shot at Alexander, Cheney, Gramm, and Kemp. That's exactly how it came across to me the first time he said it—in a context that made it clear enough we were talking about just this group of people.

"Book list" is sort of Beltway. Call and I'll explain.

I don't want to call Bennett's policy aide—who just returned today from vacation into a cauldron of activity—until we have *all* the questions we want to ask him. When will your researcher have hers?

Again, thanks for everything.

Albest,

Peter Ross Range

COMMENTS

This letter (which was faxed to me, by the way, rather than mailed because we were nearing deadline and needed the info fast) was in response to three specific questions I needed interviewer Range to answer regarding the final rewrite on his William J. Bennett interview in our March-April 1995 issue. He began with a pleasantry in response to a compliment I'd given him in my original transmission. He next got down to business by addressing each concern separately and succinctly. And finally he closed with a polite finale. I respect this kind of no-nonsense response because it acknowledges that both parties are busy people: It accomplishes its objective while not wasting either person's time.

Letters Between You and Others

Although the bulk of your writing-related correspondence will be between you and editors, you'll frequently come into contact with other individuals during the course of research-gathering and your actual assignments. These include agents, publishers, publicists, PR agencies, authorities, celebrities, witnesses, personal assistants, secretaries. In short, just about anybody.

It stands to reason, therefore, that since you need most of these "other" people to complete just about every article or story you'll ever write, your correspondence with them had better be just as professional, interesting, and to-the-point as your foremost queries. If they aren't, many easily opened doors will be unnecessarily shut—and locked. I don't have to tell you how much time is taken up by just preparation and appointment-scheduling on most writing projects. Therefore, you don't want to needlessly drag out this process with letters that don't accomplish what you want the first time out.

The actual letters I've selected below represent some of the most common situations and tasks you will encounter as a freelance writer.

"How Do I Arrange an Interview With a Celebrity?"

As an editor, I am often called upon to write politicians, executives, authorities, celebrities, writers, and other dignitaries requesting an interview or an assignment on behalf of the magazine. Of all the letters I've sent out, one particular query has elicited remarkable results. I don't know why this format has produced so many favorable responses, but I do have some theories. Can you come up with your own? Here is the version I sent to novelist and essayist John Edgar Wideman:

Dear Mr. Wideman:

I am a senior editor of *Modern Maturity*, the membership magazine for the American Association of Retired Persons (AARP), and am in charge of assigning a wide variety of special projects. I'm writing to ask if you would be interested in interviewing American Indian activist Russell Means for our new feature, the MM Interview.

The 4,000-word Q&A is patterned after the venerable *Playboy* and *Rolling Stone* versions. It is a heavyweight discourse with legends age fifty and over in the fields of entertainment, science, business, culture, government, economics, sports, the community, and the arts.

To ensure our portraits are in-depth, candid, and captivating we are approaching America's finest writers and interviewers to invite them to conduct future sessions. Yours was one of the names on my list. I have long admired your essays, your articles, your "autobiographical fiction." One writer I thought described you best: "a master story-teller, a witness, a prophet."

The latter distinction could very well fit Russell Means, a longtime Indian activist, an environmentalist, and—to slightly alter a description once made of you—"a leading chronicler of rural Indian life." Because of the similarities in your lives and experiences and struggles and causes, your name sprung sharply to my mind when I tried to think of who would be the ideal interviewer for Mr. Means.

Would you be interested in undertaking this assignment? We have sent an invitation to Mr. Means and expect to hear from him shortly. If he should decline or not be available, we have other national figures we would like to propose to you.

For your information, our circulation (more than twenty-two million) currently ranks first among all U.S. magazines. Questions and issues raised in an interview featuring John Edgar Wideman and Russell Means would therefore reach an audience unprecedented in magazine publication. *Modern Maturity*'s success and growth in the past few years has enabled us to feature the opinions of some of America's top writers, thinkers, and personalities. It would be an honor to include you in this pantheon of important contemporary figures.

Sincerely,

John Wood

Senior Editor

COMMENTS

Although this particular letter was sent to a writer, it could easily be adapted to a celebrity or other well-known person. The reasons this particular format has so often worked, I believe, are that it:

1. Sets the stage: Explain who you are, who you represent, and what you want.
2. Gives details: Explain exactly what the interview process will entail.
3. Shows interest: Tell the person specifically why you chose him or her.
4. Does its homework: Explain why the individual would be ideal for the publication you're representing.
5. Closes the sale: Ask bluntly will the person do it?
6. Brings out the numbers: In case the person is wavering about whether to accept, trot out the publication's strongest attributes—circulation, reputation, former contributors, whatever they may be. Then invite the person to join those illustrious ranks. Who could resist?

Dear Mr. Stewart:

Recently, I was given my first assignment with a national and, in this case, a worldwide-distributed magazine, *Modern Maturity*, to write an article about my favorite film, and yours, *It's A Wonderful Life*.

Modern Maturity is primarily sent to persons fifty years old and older, though many younger persons enjoy it, too; I have often read my mother's copy before she's even gotten around to looking at it! The circulation of this informative and entertaining magazine is twenty-two million and is the largest magazine in the nation. When my article is run, it will be seen by more people than I can begin to imagine. What a wonderful and important responsibility as well as a once-in-a-lifetime opportunity to share my thoughts about *It's A Wonderful Life* and to share my love for my favorite film.

Modern Maturity's editor has assigned me to write the piece and he feels, as I do, that an interview with you, "George Bailey," would make a significant contribution to the piece. I am therefore requesting the opportunity to meet with you to discuss Mr. Capra's great film. The editor's deadline for the piece is December 30, 1988, so I would hope to talk with you sometime in October, November, or December, right before Christmas, whatever time would be most convenient for you and would fit into your busy schedule.

You may remember me as the person who sent you the *It's A Wonderful Life* Christmas cards over the past several years and a birthday card that showed a tiger at the Columbus Zoo and a card this year with a horse that resembled your beloved Pie. Each time I corresponded with you, you kindly and thoughtfully acknowledged my card and I was thrilled and honored to have heard from you. It meant so much to me.

I look forward to hearing from you, Mr. Stewart, and hope we will be able to talk about *It's A Wonderful Life*. If I am able to write a piece for *Modern Maturity* that will urge its readers to watch *It's A Wonderful Life* for the first time or the twentieth time and if by seeing this film the story touches the heart of even one more person or heals and enriches the spirit of yet another person, then I truly will be "the richest woman in town," for my guardian angel would have answered my prayer. I know the warmth and delight of this film, and my friends and family and I know the faith, strength, and hope this film has to offer.

Again, Mr. Stewart, thank you for all your kindnesses.

Sincerely,

Nancy Dillon

COMMENTS

This writer's letter to Jimmy Stewart resulted in an invitation to visit the actor at his home. From their ensuing two-and-a-half hour visit, Dillon fashioned a charming article about the movie and Jimmy Stewart, not to mention childhood, faith, redemption, love, and holiday cheer—in short, a perfect piece for Christmas. "A Celluloid Dream" appeared in our December-January 1989-1990 issue.

How do you request a follow-up interview with a celebrity you've already talked to? In the letter below, writer Claudia Dreifus wrote PBS host Bill Moyers and asked for an extra interview session on our behalf.

Dear Bill:

Welcome back from your travels.

As you may recall, when we spoke over the winter we spoke a little about questions of aging. At the time, you were contemplating a series, "The Wisdom of the Elders," and you had shot some material with Agnes DeMille.

With that in mind, I edited the out-takes from *TV Guide* for *Modern Maturity*. In that interview are some thoughts on aging as you gave them in December, more material on "Healing and the Mind," some historic material on Lyndon Johnson. Everything went through and was accepted.

Last week I got a desperate call from my editor there: "It's got to be updated by next week. It has to go into the October-November issue. Otherwise, there's no room for Moyers for another year."

In magazines, when something remains in-house for a full year, it usually dies.

Moreover, this editor sent me his edit of my piece—with fill-in questions and requests for additional material on aging.

Can I prevail on you for a half hour—either on the phone or in person? Even if the series has not yet sold to PBS . . . we'd like to talk about broader issues of wisdom of the elders.

The deadline for the copy to be set in type is the end of this week.

Best,

Claudia Dreifus

COMMENTS

This seat-of-the-pants type example won't come into play that often with most writers, but it shows that, even with high-powered celebrities, simply coming clean and talking straight will often do the trick. She got the session with the very busy Moyers within the week, the new material was superb, and her interview appeared in our October-November 1993 issue. (Note: You keen freelancers out there will have already picked up on how this enterprising writer managed to deftly sell two big-money articles from one interview assignment!)

"How Do I Arrange an Interview With a Noncelebrity?"

You probably write lots of these letters. For one article assignment alone, you may be required to interview a dozen or more people—taxi drivers, shop owners, racetrack bettors, friends of the deceased, etc. Average, everyday people. How do you contact them? By phone or letter. Many writers pick up the phone first because it's easier and faster. But even when you do that, the person may request a letter first to "spell out" in writing what you have in mind.

Since you're dealing with normal folk here and not Hollywood, Congressional, or any other kind of royalty—and since most of these people will probably constitute the background of your article rather than its focal point, you won't need to shovel the you-know-what so thick. Here is a letter one of our editors sent to a prison inmate whom we wanted to interview for a crime story. You could easily adapt this to your own usage (i.e., rewrite it so it's coming from you, not an editor):

Dear Mr. Torres:

I am an associate editor at *Modern Maturity*, the membership magazine for the American Association of Retired Persons (AARP). I am writing to ask if you would participate in a story we are doing on the mugging incident involving you and Mr. Kern that took place on January 9, 1994.

Unlike the typical newspaper stories that are written about incidents like yours, we want to reenact the event and report its aftermath from the points of view of all the parties involved—each individual is an essential piece of the whole "puzzle." We would like to give you the opportunity to tell your story to one of our writers, to ensure that your side is clearly and accurately presented. We would make the necessary calls to arrange the interview. The other parties involved in your case have all agreed to work with us.

I hope you also agree to help us compile the best story possible. We are working on a fairly tight deadline so I'd appreciate a reply as soon as possible. You can call me collect at [phone number] or write me at [address]. I hope to hear from you soon. Thank you.

Sincerely,

Leslie Yap

COMMENTS

The differences between this and the letter above to a celebrity are that in this case (1) you don't have to proclaim the prestige or reputation or circulation of the publication to get the person to commit (regular people are thrilled to appear anywhere in print); (2) you don't have to heap praise on the person to get a commitment (whereas you'd better do so with a major personality); (3) you don't have to detail what the assignment will entail (a car mechanic won't care as much as Elizabeth Taylor about the questions you're going to ask or how long the interview may take); and (4) you don't have to be so formal; you can just talk like you would with your next-door neighbor.

"How Do I Request a Press Trip or Obtain a Press Pass for an Event?"

Before you can write about anything, you need to know firsthand what you're writing about. If you want to do a story on mule trips down the Grand Canyon, it doesn't take a rocket scientist to know that at some point you're going to have go to the Grand Canyon and hop on ol' Dixie, who reeks of dust and turnips and tends to bite. Same goes if you want to cover an upcoming jazz concert for your local newspaper. It would help your review immensely if you were actually there.

So how do you get these plumb assignments? That would take an entire book to outline. But basically, the writers you see at these events have probably spent years schmoozing with the people associated with them, or they have worked on various projects connected with the affairs. Or they're affiliated with the trade industry that organizes the events. Or they've covered similar happenings or gone to similar locales. In short, there are probably as many ways to gain credentials as there are things to write about or places to go.

One way is to phone or meet the person in charge of publicity and/or tourism for the event/ tour you're interested in. Then follow up with a detailed letter on yourself and your assignment. Here is a good example from travel writer and radio host, Joseph Rosendo, who wrote the head of the Mississippi Commission for International Cultural Exchange requesting a press trip:

Dear Mr. Kyle:

It was a pleasure speaking with you this morning. As promised, enclosed is information on "Travelscope."

For ten years I have produced and hosted "Travelscope," California's all-travel radio show. The show broadcasts Saturdays and Sundays on stations KIEV 870AM Los Angeles and KNRY 1240AM Monterey. "Travelscopes' " ninety-minute format includes segments such as Dateline: The World; California Getaways; and Food, Wine, and Travel Hotlines that frequently highlight national and historic destinations.

"Travelscope" also airs on the Cable Radio Network heard on one hundred cable television systems and in eight million homes nationwide, including Northern and Southern California.

As a travel journalist and photographer, I have had articles and photos published in major newspapers and magazines nationwide, including the *Los Angeles Times*, the *Washington Post*, the *New York Daily News*, the *Chicago Sun-Times*, and *Westways*, *Vista*, and *Dynamic Years* magazines. I am a member of the International Food, Wine & Travel Writers Association and the National Association of Radio Talk Show Hosts.

I also produce the bimonthly *Travelscope* publication for six thousand readers. The publication includes travel features, bargains, and tips on consumer travel topics in such columns as "Resorts, Hotels, and Inns"; "Anchors Aweigh"; and "Planes, Trains, Etc."

Both the radio show and publication feature major travel destinations. When I return from a trip I dispense with my guest/call-in format and devote a large portion of the show to that destination or trip. I bring back to "Travelscope" the local sounds and excitement, as well as my personal tips on how to get the most out of the experience.

As host and producer of "Travelscope" and publisher of *Travelscope*, I have no difficulty in featuring the hosting airlines, restaurants, hotels, etc. on the radio and in the publication.

Based on the information we discussed, I am particularly interested in your Russia press trip in August. In addition, I am doing my best to rearrange my schedule to make one of your Mississippi trips.

If you have any questions, please call me. I look forward to working with you. Immediately upon receiving word regarding whether I can change the dates on my live remote broadcast originally scheduled for April 8, I will call you.

Best regards,

Joseph Rosendo

Producer/Host/Publisher

"Travelscope"

COMMENTS

Event organizers and tourist promoters want to know only one thing from you: How many ways from Sunday can you hype my event/destination? They get tons of letters from FFFFs (freelancers fishing for freebies) who write in and say, "I'm a travel writer and if you let me go to Russia or Mississippi, I'll write a story about it." They know that already. They want to know how plugged in you are to the media community. Do you have connections to publishers or other outlets? Do you have an assignment? Do you write a column? What's your track record on these sorts of junkets? Don't be afraid to overwhelm a promoter with your credits, ideas, and opportunities. This may be your one shot in life for that fantasy trip to Bora Bora—all expenses paid.

What promoters rarely get are letters like this one, which precisely and voluminously detail what the writer plans to do with the material and all the ways in which the writer's participation could benefit the promoting organization. If you were the destination organizer, which writer would *you* award the free ticket to?

"How Do I Request Information From Someone?"

You may need to obtain many things during the course of an assignment—data, publications, documents, referrals, factual verification, etc. You can call or write for most information. If you write, keep these fifteen factors in mind:

1. Make your letter as brief as possible. The more precise you are, the more likely your request will be honored.

2. Write to an individual, not an institution or a title. Otherwise, your request may get lost in the bureaucratic labyrinth.

3. Declare what you want in the very first sentence. Don't waste the busy reader's time explaining why you want it before you state what you want.

4. Be specific about what you want. Don't just ask for "any information you have." A company may have reams of data on your topic or hundreds of brochures on their products.

5. If you're requesting many items, arrange them in the form of numbered questions rather than bunching everything into the same paragraph. This way the recipient can check each one off and be assured that they'll all be accounted for.

6. Tell the reader who you are and why you need it.

7. Act grateful for whatever the recipient can provide rather than implying or demanding that you have a right to the material.

8. Request your favor matter-of-factly. Don't say, "I'm sorry to bother you." There's no need to be apologetic because it's normal to ask for things.

9. State exactly what you want your reader to do.

10. Make it easy for the recipient. If you're requesting permission to use copyrighted material, for example, include a copy of your letter that the person can just sign, date, and return.

11. Explain why it's in your reader's interest to respond.

12. Tell the reader where to send or transmit the information.

13. Specify the date by which you need the material.

14. Express your thanks for any help your reader may provide. But don't just say "Thank you"; this implies an end to the communication. Instead, give an appreciation for the expected cooperation: "A quote from you would be appreciated" or "Thank you for your anticipated cooperation."

15. Enclose an SASE, if appropriate.

Professor Wilson:

Would you please read the accompanying pages for accuracy?

The article is scheduled for our May-June issue. Ordinarily we would use a tape transcript to check your quotes, but one of the writer's tapes was defective and we wanted to make sure we've quoted you correctly.

I've asked some specific questions (see separate page), but please feel free to comment on or correct any part of the article. I hope you can reply by February 2.

Thank you for your consideration of this request.

COMMENTS

This letter was sent by a researcher to an expert quoted in an article, but it could just as easily have been sent by you to an expert quoted in *your* article. The letter's brevity, graciousness, and professionalism greased the wheels of this transaction, and the information was sent back in time to meet the deadline.

Questions & Answers

Q: I've worked with one particular editor several times now. When, if ever, is it appropriate to switch my letters to a more informal style?

A: Some writers believe they've reached the inner sanctum of a publication when they surpass the prestigious two dollars per word plateau; others when they're awarded a "contributing editor" slot. But the ones who really know what it's all about don't believe they've made it until they can confidently address their editor by his or her first name followed by a comma—or "Bubba" followed by whatever they want.

Seriously, though, you can never go wrong if you follow an editor's lead (never lead yourself). Most editors, once a relationship has been established, gradually tend to lighten up on the salutation. The colon might be the first to go, replaced by a comma. Next will probably come the first name supplanting the Mr./Mrs./Ms. What if you've sold several pieces to the same editor and have a jovial rapport with her on the phone—but she still addresses you as "Dear Mr. Williams:" each time she writes? You've clearly got a stuffy editor from the old school. In that case, just keep on addressing her as "Dear Ms. Jones:" and don't fret; it's not you.

Q: Is faxing an editor improper?

A: On most types of correspondence, a standard letter is preferred; it carries more weight and respect and delight. There's something about getting a personally addressed envelope with a crisp, clean letter inside. A fax, although coming across as more urgent, rarely is. It's crude, grungy, and impersonal. Plus you have to go down to the end of the hall where the machine is to get it, and it's lying there exposed for everyone to see—from the boss to the clean-up crew.

Nevertheless, there are times when a fax is more appropriate than a letter: If an editor calls you and requests something immediately, if you need to update an editor during an assignment, or if you just want to send a short, but urgent, note.

Never, however, send a faxed query. Writers seem to have instinctively picked up that this mode of communication is anathema to editors because although there must be tens of thousands of freelancers out there with fax machines, our office received probably less than a dozen faxed queries in 1994. Faxed queries can't come with SASEs, so right there you're doomed. Do you expect an editor to fax you back a reject letter? The time and bureaucracy involved in just sending back an SASE is bad enough; but to expect an overworked and underpaid editorial assistant—or the overworked and underpaid editor herself—to line up at the fax machine down the hall with everybody else and personally send you—and everyone else who sent one—a form letter back is unrealistic.

Bibliography

Richard H. Beatty. *175 High-Impact Cover Letters*. John Wiley & Sons, Inc.: 1992

Richard H. Beatty. *The Perfect Cover Letter*. John Wiley & Sons: 1989

Lassor A. Blumenthal. *The Art of Letter Writing: The New Guide to Writing More Effective Letters for All Occasions*. Grosset: 1977

John Boswell. *The Awful Truth About Publishing*. Warner Books: 1986

Gordon Burgett. *How to Sell More Than 75 Percent of Your Freelance Writing*. Prima Publishing: 1990

Gordon Burgett. *Query Letters, Cover Letters: How They Sell Your Writing*.

Communication Unlimited: 1985

Lisa Collier Cool. *How to Write Irresistible Query Letters*. Writer's Digest Books: 1987

Richard Curtis. *Beyond the Bestseller: A Literary Agent Takes You Inside the Book Business*. New American Library: 1989

Diane Gage and Marcia Hibsch Coppess Price. *Get Published! Top Magazine Editors Tell You How*. Stern Sloan: 1986

Gerald Gross. Editors *On Editing: What Writers Need to Know About What Editors Do*. Grove Press: 1993

Jeff Herman. *Insider's Guide to Book Editors, Publishers and Literary Agents*. Prima Publishing: 1992

Ronald L. Krannich & Caryl Rae Krannich. *Dyamite Cover Letters*. Impact Publication: 1992

Rosalie Maggio. *How to Say It: Choice Words, Phrases, Sentences and Paragraphs for Every Situation*. Prentice-Hall: 1990

Harold E. Meyer. *Lifetime Encyclopedia of Letters*. Prentice-Hall: 1992

Linda B. Sturgeon & Anne R. Hagler. *Personal Letters That Mean Business*. Prentice-Hall: 1991

Michael C. Thomsett. *The Little Black Book of Business Letters*. American Management Association: 1988

Index

More Great Books for Writers!

1996 Writer's Market—Celebrating 75 years of helping writers realize their dreams, this newest edition contains information on 4,000 writing opportunities. You'll find all the facts vital to the success of your writing career, including an up-to-date listing of buyers of books, articles and stories, listings of contests and awards, plus articles and interviews with top professionals. *#10432/$27.99/1008 pages*

The Writer's Ultimate Research Guide—Save research time and frustration with the help of this guide. Three hundred fifty-two information-packed pages will point you straight to the information you need to create better, more accurate fiction and nonfiction. With hundreds of listings of books and databases, each entry reveals how current the information is, what the content and organization is like and much more! *#10447/$19.99/352 pages*

How to Write Like an Expert About Anything—Find out how to use new technology and traditional research methods to get the information you need, envision new markets and write proposals that sell, find and interview experts on any topic and much more! *#10449/$17.99/224 pages*

How to Write Fast (While Writing Well)—Discover what makes a story and what it takes to research and write one. Then, learn step by step how to cut wasted time and effort by planning interviews for maximum results, beating writer's block with effective plotting, getting the most information from traditional library research and on-line computer data bases and much more! Plus, a complete chapter loaded with tricks and tips for faster writing. *#10473/$15.99/208 pages/paperback*

How to Write Irresistible Query Letters—Don't shortchange your idea with a lukewarm query! Cool shows how to select a strong slant, hook an editor with a tantalizing lead, sell yourself as the expert for the job and more. *#10146/$10.95/136 pages/paperback*

Make Your Words Work—Loaded with samples and laced with exercises, this guide will help you clean up your prose, refine your style, strengthen your descriptive powers, bring music to your words and much more! *#10399/$14.99/304 pages/paperback*

The Best Writing on Writing, Volume 2—This year's best collection of memorable essays, book excerpts and lectures on fiction, nonfiction, poetry, screenwriting and the writing life. *#48013/$16.99/224 pages/paperback*

30 Steps to Becoming a Writer and Getting Published—This informational and inspirational guide helps you get started as a writer, develops your skills and style and gets your work ready for submission. *#10367/$16.99/176 pages*

The Fiction Dictionary—The essential guide to the inside language of fiction. You'll discover genres you've never explored, writing devices you'll want to attempt, fresh characters to populate your stories. *The Fiction Dictionary* dusts off the traditional concept of "dictionary" by giving full, vivid descriptions, and by using lively examples from classic and contemporary fiction . . . turning an authoritative reference into a can't-put-it-down browser. *#48008/$18.99/336 pages*

1996 Novel & Short Story Writer's Market—Get the information you need to get your short stories and novels published. You'll discover listings on fiction publishers, plus original articles on fiction writing techniques; detailed subject categories to help you target appropriate publishers; and interviews with writers, publishers and editors! *#10441/$22.99/624 pages*

Handbook of Short Story Writing, Volume II—Orson Scott Card, Dwight V. Swain, Kit Reed and other noted authors bring you sound advice and timeless techniques for every aspect of the writing process. *#10239/$14.99/252 pages/paperback*

Creating Characters: How to Build Story People—Grab the empathy of your reader with characters so real they'll jump off the page. You'll discover how to make characters come alive with vibrant emotion, quirky personality traits, inspiring heroism, tragic weaknesses and other uniquely human qualities. *#10417/$14.99/192 pages/paperback*

Description—Discover how to use detailed description to awaken the reader's senses; advance the story using only relevant description; create original word depictions of people, animals, places, weather and much more! *#10451/$15.99/176 pages*

The Writer's Digest Guide to Good Writing—In one book, you'll find the best in writing instruction gleaned from the past 75 years of *Writer's Digest* magazine! Successful authors like Vonnegut, Steinbeck, Oates, Michener and over a dozen others share their secrets on writing technique, idea generation, inspiration and getting published. *#10391/$18.99/352 pages*

The Wordwatcher's Guide to Good Writing and Grammar—Avoid embarrassing grammar mistakes with this handy volume. Freeman gives hundreds of examples to clarify word usage, meaning, spelling and pronunciation. *#10197/$16.99/320 pages/paperback*

The Craft of Writing Science Fiction That Sells—You'll discover how to fascinate audiences (and attract editors) with imaginative, well-told science fiction. Bova shows you how to market your ideas, submit your manuscripts and more! *#10395/$16.95/224 pages*

The Writer's Digest Guide to Manuscript Formats—Don't take chances with your hard work! Learn how to prepare and submit books, poems, scripts, stories and more with the professional look editors expect from a good writer. *#10025/$19.99/200 pages*

Fiction Writer's Workshop—Explore each aspect of the art of fiction including point of view, description, revision, voice and more. At the end of each chapter you'll find more than a dozen writing exercises to help you put what you've learned into action. *#48003/$17.99/256 pages*

Write Tight: How to Keep Your Prose Sharp, Focused and Concise—Discover how to say exactly what you want with grace and power, using not only the right word, but also the right number of words. Specific instructions and helpful exercises explain and demonstrate the process for you. *#10360/$16.99/192 pages*

Beginning Writer's Answer Book—This book answers 900 of the most often asked questions about every stage of the writing process. You'll find business advice, tax tips, plus new information about on-line networks, databases and more. *#10394/$17.99/336 pages*

Writing for Money—Discover where to look for writing opportunities—and how to make them pay off. You'll learn how to write for magazines, newspapers, radio and TV, newsletters, greeting cards and a dozen other hungry markets! *#10425/$17.99/256 pages*

Voice & Style—Discover how to create character and story voices! You'll learn to write with a spellbinding narrative voice, create original character voices, write dialogue that conveys personality, control tone of voice to create mood and make the story's voices harmonize into a solid style. *#10452/$15.99/176 pages*

Writing Mysteries—Sue Grafton weaves the experience of today's top mystery authors into a mystery writing "how-to." You'll learn how to create great mystery, including making stories more taut, more immediate and more fraught with tension. *#10286/$18.99/204 pages*

Roget's Superthesaurus—For whenever you need just the right word! You'll find "vocabulary builder" words with pronunciation keys and sample sentences, quotations that double as synonyms, plus the only word-find reverse dictionary in any thesaurus—all in alphabetical format! *#10424/$22.99/624 pages*

Freeing Your Creativity: A Writer's Guide—Discover how to escape the traps that stifle your creativity. You'll tackle techniques for banishing fears and nourishing ideas so you can get your juices flowing again. *#10430/$14.99/176 pages/paperback*

Manuscript Submission—After you create a timely and thought-provoking work, you need to take that last step toward getting published—submitting your manuscript. This guide shows you how to WOW editors by submitting a manuscript with the look and format of a true professional. *#10156/$14.99/176 pages*

The Complete Guide to Magazine Article Writing—You'll write articles that are clear, focused, effective and best of all, salable, with the practical explanations and easy-to-follow instructions in this comprehensive guide. *#10369/$17.99/304 pages*

Writing the Blockbuster Novel—Let a top-flight agent show you how to weave the essential elements of a blockbuster into your own novels with memorable characters, exotic settings, clashing conflicts and more! *#10393/$18.99/224 pages*

How to Write a Book Proposal—Don't sabotage your great ideas with a so-so proposal. This guide includes a complete sample proposal, a nine-point Idea Test to check the salability of your book ideas, plus hot tips to make your proposal a success! *#10173/$12.99/136 pages/paperback*

Plot—Don't let your novel or short story sag in the middle or fizzle out at the end. Dibell shares dozens of secrets and techniques for building and sustaining gripping, memorable plots. *#10044/$14.99/176 pages*

The 29 Most Common Writing Mistakes and How to Avoid Them—Weak comparisons, too many adjectives, excessive self-expression—with clarity and good humor, Delton shows how to correct these and 26 other common writing mistakes to help you get published! *#10221/$9.95/96 pages/paperback*

Writing the Short Story: A Hands-On Program—With Bickham's unique "workshop on paper" you'll plan, organize, write, revise and polish a short story. Clear instruction, helpful charts and practical exercises will lead you every step of the way! *#10421/$16.99/224 pages*

Writing the Novel: From Plot to Print—Block, author of more than 100 published novels, answers the questions that plague both novice and experienced novelists and leads you step by step toward getting published. *#02747/$11.95/218 pages/paperback*

The Complete Guide to Writing Fiction—This concise guide will help you develop the skills you need to write and sell long and short fiction. You'll get a complete rundown on outlining, narrative writing details, description, pacing and action. *#10158/$18.95/312 pages*

20 Master Plots (And How to Build Them)—Write great contemporary fiction from timeless plots. This guide outlines 20 plots from various genres and illustrates how to adapt them into your own fiction. *#10366/$17.99/240 pages*

Conflict, Action & Suspense—Discover how to grab your reader with an action-packed beginning, build the suspense throughout your story and bring it all to a fever pitch through powerful, gripping conflict. *#10396/$14.99/176 pages*

The Writer's Guide to Everyday Life in the Middle Ages—This time-travel companion will guide you through the medieval world of Northwestern Europe. Discover the facts on dining habits, clothing, armor, festivals, religious orders and much more—everything you need to paint an authentic picture. *#10423/$17.99/256 pages*

The Writer's Guide to Everyday Life from Prohibition through World War II—Uncover all the details you need to add color, depth and a ring-of-truth to your work. You'll find an intimate look at what life was like back then, including popular slang, the Prohibition, the Depression, World War II, crime, transportation, fashion, radio, music and much more! *#10450/$18.99/272 pages*

Police Procedural: A Writer's Guide to the Police and How They Work—Learn how police officers work, when they work, what they wear, who they report to and how they go about controlling and investigating crime. *#10374/$16.99/272 pages/paperback*

Private Eyes: A Writer's Guide to Private Investigators—How do people become investigators? What procedures do they use? What tricks/tactics do they use? This guide gives you the "inside scoop" on the world of private eyes! *#10373/$15.99/208 pages/ paperback*

Scene of the Crime: A Writer's Guide to Crime-Scene Investigation—Save time with this quick reference book! You'll find loads of facts and details on how police scour crime scenes for tell-tale clues. *#10319/$15.99/240 pages/paperback*